None But The Brave

Hamblen Sears

Printing Statement:

Due to the very old age and scarcity of this book,
many of the pages may be hard to read due to the
blurring of the original text, possible missing pages,
missing text, dark backgrounds and other issues
beyond our control.

Because this is such an important and rare work, we
believe it is best to reproduce this book regardless of
its original condition.

Thank you for your understanding.

None but the Brave

By Hamblen Sears

NEW YORK
DODD MEAD & COMPANY
MDCCCCII

THE CAXTON PRESS
NEW YORK.

" We turned . . . into the main highway of the Hudson "

CONTENTS

♥ CONTENTS ♥

LIST OF ILLUSTRATIONS

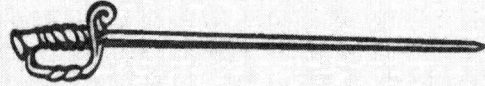

None but the Brave —

I DO not know why I should sit here to write of my earlier days. There was nothing in them out of the ordinary, as I look back at them now; nothing but what might, and no doubt did, happen to many another young fellow in those busy days of our great fight for the right to live as we deemed best in this new land across the sea. And yet those days did then seem to me unusual, and I can tell the youngsters that come after me that there was something to be done every hour, and many a goodly thrust of sword and pike to make for what was our right and our just due. Thank God, the long years are gone that devastated this fair land and destroyed the happiness of so many families! And when I think of the ruined towns and the thousands of graves left by that long war, I cannot help bidding those who come after us to give their forbears what is but their due — the credit for making a free land with their blood, and leaving a bit of this green earth where the next that come to it may breathe the air of freedom.

Perhaps in this year of our Lord, 1811, the grave signs of another disagreement with Great Britain makes me want to do my share to ward off another

fight, by telling the men of to-day something of the
struggle we had thirty and more years ago. In good
truth, if the hotheads have not a care we shall be at
it again, and no mistake. And yet, if the time should
again come, if a second struggle is to be fought out,
then this hand that scratches across the page now is
not so weak, nor the heart so sluggish, but that I can
take the old sword down from my study wall and
strike another blow for the rocks and hills and homes
we worked so hard to call our own, back in the last
century. Let the men of England make no mistake!
Those of us who are getting on towards the three
score of years have still the spark in us, and we can
stand up beside the younger ones, who have come
since the old days, and mayhap show them a point or
two that came to us from the great Washington.

Perhaps, though, this itch of the pen comes only
from a wish to recall those strenuous days, when my
friends and I lived a life that could not be equalled
for its constant change and its constant action. Those
were great old times, when we saw little of the misery
and much of the famous fighting, when we worked
out the beginnings of what we now call American.

Perhaps, yet once again, it is all to recall the face
that is not a hundred miles from me at this moment,
that has walked and worked by my side these thirty
years. Aye, friend, if you had but known her then
— if you but knew her now — the fearless gentle
nature that has made me what I am, that would have
made me so much more had I been aught but a lump
of animated clay! If you could but have looked into

her eyes and seen what I saw! If you could but have heard her voice! — hark! I can hear it now — that old song somewhere above stairs, as she goes about her daily work of bringing up the chickens she and I are trying to make worthy their native land. Chickens they are no longer, but sturdy boys and girls — men and women they would call themselves. Yet their father, sitting here in his study looking out on Boston Common, could tell them a tale — aye, has many a time, in part, — that would wake the brave spirit in them.

Well, whatever the reason for this scribbling, I have a liking for trying it. Perhaps it may stir up some lad. Perhaps it may give a hint to some young girl as to what a woman was in those days, and should be in these. Indeed, I believe I have it now! 'T is the last reason, to be sure! For as I walk down old Beacon Hill and along the Charles after a useless day of voting in the House to widen my neighbor's street or some such meaningless trash, and come upon one of the fairest of all God's creations — as I see her walking onward in all the innocence and beauty of her youth, there must needs come into these eyes of mine weak tears to think that I am old, and yet that I have seen the time when such as she would send me smiling to my grave could I but keep her just as she is in her fearlessness and gentleness and youth. And, indeed, if need be, I can do it now; for fifty winters cannot so change a man that he should forget that.

But, such as it is, here is the story.

CHAPTER I

'TIS a simple tale, yet not an uneventful one. And as I sit here and bite the end of my quill, I can see again a dirty night in '80, thirty years ago, a warm, late September evening with the fine rain tumbling down on the leaves of the trees that bordered the road. The pattering drops, the thump of Roger's hoofs as he kept on his steady gait with bowed head and bedraggled mane, the occasional loom of a big maple, and the sense of wretchedness and loneliness were the only sounds and thoughts that came to my consciousness.

Yet back of it all was that constant watchfulness that, young as I was, I had learned always to have by me, — a lesson common to all who had served with General Putnam for a year or two. The vigorous old man had given me many a parting caution as he shook me heartily by the hand, telling me to have a care of this Hudson River country and of the wild thieves that broke out with fine impartiality upon colonial and king's soldiers alike. And thus I had ridden out of Connecticut and turned up the river in the midst of the silent, gloomy September rain.

It must have been eight or nine o'clock, for darkness comes on early in such a country on such a night, and I had had many an anxious quarter of an hour since nightfall looking for the tavern that, according to my information, should be about here anywhere.

Suddenly I became aware of a light ahead in the middle of the road, evidently not from any tavern window, but from an ordinary coach lantern, moving here and there so strangely that instinctively Roger slowed up, and allowed me to guide him in under the trees to one side.

A moment's observation showed me a huge and, so far as could be told in that light, fine family coach tilted at such an unnatural angle that I perceived it to be in distress. Two men were at work upon the wheel, or rather standing about examining it, and, nothing appearing amiss, I rode up quietly and asked them what had befallen them.

" Misery enough," growled a churlish voice in reply. " Here we be stranded in the country with never a nail nor strap to help us."

I liked not his tone nor his manner, and probably showed as much in my reply, for he straightened, and I saw him feel at his belt.

" That is not much, you say, do you? " he cried. " And do you think that all? "

" Tut, tut, my friend. Take your hand from your belt and tell me what have you inside."

" God knows! " he answered with renewed wrath. " A witch, a woman, the devil, perhaps; " and added,

"Settle your head well on your shoulders before you go nigh to that door!"

As I approached the coach, a hooded head appeared at the window, and a high girlish voice said in a strain just betwixt uncontrollable anger and tears:

"You wretched men, cannot something be done? Am I to die here in this dreadful night? Who are you, sir?"

"A wanderer, madam, at your service," I answered.

"Thank God for a human voice with some temper to it," she cried. "Can you not whip these churls into doing something, sir?"

I could not fail to notice even then that, afraid though she might be, anger controlled her more than fear.

"The case is not so bad, mistress, as you think. We cannot be more than a mile from Gowan's Tavern, which stands hereabouts."

"But how am I to get there?"

"If you could mount my horse, we would make it in a short time, with only a little worse wetting."

Thereupon without reason the note changed.

"I cannot! I cannot!" said she with tears in her voice.

"If you will trust to me —"

"And who are you?" she cried suddenly. "I do not know you."

Somewhat nettled at these abrupt changes of manner, I was guilty of pique. Wherefore, answering that I had but tried to offer her help, I made as if to move on.

"Wait! Wait! In God's name, sir, would you leave me here in such a wilderness?"

"Indeed, I would not, mistress, but it appears you do not wish my help."

Thereupon the door opened, and a chit of a creature in a black hood and long cape stepped out and down into nearly a foot of mud.

I was off Roger in an instant, and by her side.

"Forgive me, young lady; I was as rude as your men. Come, the thing is not so bad;" and without more ado, for, to tell gospel truth, the thought of her little feet in that oozing mud gave me confidence, I picked her up as if she had been a baby and set her on old Roger's back.

"And do you two men unhitch the horses and lead them on after us to the tavern," I added.

The havoc created by the mud was evident enough now, for as I led my horse by the lantern I could see a tiny shoe that once had had a bright silver buckle. But its shimmer was dim now under the dripping yellow mud, and, as far as I could see, the same clay covered what must have been a black silk stocking. Then in a moment I had led Roger out of the light and up the road.

Here was a pretty mess. What would the general say to his emissary to the Commander-in-Chief, so carefully cautioned to avoid any embarrassment, to steer clear of aught that might embroil him in delays? What would he say to me now, trudging along on this wretched night, the rain falling and the mud rising, leading a horse that bore a burden dropped from I knew not where and clogging my progress in this ridiculous fashion? The thought of the rain made me turn instinctively, and, taking my cape coat from my back, lean up and throw it over my companion's shoulders. But it had no sooner touched her than she cried out:

"I will not wear it! You need it, and I have a thick cape."

"You will be drenched to the skin in no time," I said firmly, as I held it in place.

"If you do not take it instantly, sir, I will throw it in the mud," she answered.

I walked along without a word. It seemed that this little baggage had the power to irritate me beyond measure.

"Will you take it?" she cried, in a vibrant voice.

"No, I will not," I exclaimed, in quite as defiant a tone.

"Oh, very well!" said she, and therewith tossed my best, my only coat into the Tarrytown mire, as if it had been the peel of an orange.

I stopped a moment with anger that was on the point of bursting forth. Then I stooped, picked up the coat, threw it over my shoulders, and strode up to Roger's head, walking on in silence. God knows I knew little or nothing of women, never having seen many, never having known any well, for my mother had died when I was a boy, and sisters had I none. But I never suspected women of such behaviour as this, and the knowledge was anything but pleasant.

I would then and there gladly have left her alone with Roger if I had dared. What was I to do? What could I do on arrival at the tavern? And then my thoughts turned to discover the method I should pursue to get rid of my strange burden. I would wait until the arrival of her servants and then leave, go on to some other point, bad night as it was — anything to get myself up towards Fishkill and alone.

Here was I, Merton Balfort, of Putnam's division, walking up the Hudson River, leading a bedraggled woman in the worst of nights to a mythical inn, which might not exist at all for aught I knew, in a country overrun with Skinners — I, on a mission to General Washington, the importance of which I could only gather from Putnam's instructions when he gave me the letter and told me how much speed and sagacity meant.

"Is it very muddy?"

I could scarcely recognise the voice, it had so changed. All the tears, all the fear, seemed to have disappeared, and in their place something strange, very strange, had come.

"Oh, no, madam; the road is clear as a floor, and the sun is fast drying up my wet clothes," I answered, too angry, too worried, to be even civil.

I heard a slight sound as of the sudden drawing in of breath, but no other response came as we moved slowly on, until at a bend of the road we came suddenly upon the tavern, as the creaking sign over the door designated — a small, common-looking house rambling off against the side of a hill in as forsaken and silent a spot as ever villain selected for foul deed. There was nothing for it, however, but to alight, and in a moment, with neither word nor look, she had slipped off Roger's back and walked straight into the main room of the hostelry, and I after her.

CHAPTER II

IN WHICH THE WORLD ENDS FOR ONE MAN AND
BEGINS FOR ANOTHER

THE scene that met our gaze as we got through the door was anything but consoling. In fact, my companion drew back against me as she entered, and instinctively grasped my arm. For the room, which at best was about what might have been expected from the exterior of the house, was now filled with the fumes of foul tobacco; and the long, low ceiling was black with the smoke of lamps that spluttered and smelt till the atmosphere turned the gorge.

At one end burned a fire in a huge fireplace. Two or three common tables were in the room, and around one of these half a dozen men stood holding their mugs high in the air as they reeled about and sang in drunken discord:

> "For he's a cho-l-l-y good *fel*-lo-o-w!
> F'r he's a cho-l-l-y good *fel*-lo-o-w!
> F'r he's a cho-l-l-y good fel-elo-*o-o-o-w*,
> As no-body ca-an de-e-ny-y-y!"

It was clear enough that the jolly good fellow on this occasion was a wretched lump of clay lying in a most inhuman posture under the table. At the farther end of the room stood a bench, which, from the

bottles upon it, was evidently the bar, and behind this
leaned the tavern-keeper, thumping out the time with
a pewter mug.

As the company appeared to take not the slightest
notice of us, but continued to celebrate the virtues of
their for the time departed friend, I led my companion over to the fireplace, drew up a stool for her, and
bade her sit quietly for the double purpose of drying
her clothing and avoiding any unnecessary attention
from the other occupants of the room. Then, still
moving quietly, I approached the landlord, and, with
many a misgiving, asked him for some sort of food
and drink.

"Aye, food there is none," cried he; "but you can
drink yourself to death, an you will, my friend."

And forthwith he pointed to a row of ale kegs.

"Listen to me, landlord," said I sternly. "I have
a lady here, and she must have food and lodging this
night —"

I got no further, for he began thumping upon his
bar and shouted to the revellers:

"Hi, boys, look here! What in hell's name do ye
now! Stop yer screaming and howling! Do yer not
see there's gentry present?"

The noise ceased in a moment, and the company
stood looking at the tavern-keeper, and then, following the line of his finger, all turned like automatons
to where the girl sat bending over the fire. I had an
instant to study them closer, and became aware, as
one will in the twinkling of an eye, that one of the
company appeared to be of a better sort. He wore

"The room . . . was now filled with the fumes of foul tobacco".

top-boots and riding breeks and a swallow-tail coat, befouled with mud, and by his side hung a long sword. Another was a sombre, long-faced country-man, while the rest appeared to be clowns, that are alike whether in town or country the world over.

The silence lasted but an instant, and then he of the riding boots straightened himself and cried out:

"Why, you whelps of Satan, do you not know a lady has graced our board?" And, as I sidled over to the fireplace, he rolled this way and that, and finally came close to her as she turned to look at him.

"Madam," said he, as he started to make a pro-found bow with a sweep of his pewter mug, sending a thin line of ale in a circle over the floor, "mad'm, I s'lute ye — "

But the bow was too much for him, and he stumbled over his own feet, and fell at hers. The quick turn of her head, as she stepped back from him, threw her hood back on her hair, and then I saw her face for the first time.

What a face it was! I shall never forget it, never! I could not describe it; for it seemed then all eyes and wavy brown hair, and a small mouth, that had more of scorn in it than I could have believed pos-sible in any human feature. Beautiful? Aye, that it was, white now as snow, in its frame of dark hair and darker hood. But I know not what devilish influence the face had on me, for, as the man struggled to his feet, she gave him a slow look, and then, turning to me, said quietly, with contempt in her voice:

"Will you not protect me, sir?"

And I, without hesitation, struck the fool in his face with my closed fist and sent him rolling over himself against the wall.

'T was a foolhardy thing to do, and I knew it before I had finished. For, no sooner was he down, than a howl set up from the others, as they made for us. There was but time to push one of the long tables between us and to draw my rapier, when the crew was at the other side of the low barrier.

Yet then I felt more tranquil than I had since entering the tavern; for the affair was taking on the look of a fight, and I had been in so many, large and small, of late, that there was a certain familiarity to it, and it put me more at my ease. I turned the pistol out of the nearest man's hand with my point, and got the girl behind me, when the leader (for so he was) got upon his feet, purple with rage, and roared:

"Stop there! The man has insulted me! Stop! This is not for you, clowns! Clear away here!" And with a soberness I had little expected, he scattered them to either side, and, leaning his hands on the table, spluttered in my teeth:

"You, sir! You have struck me in the face! Are ye a coward, or will ye settle this here now?"

"Nothing could be better," I answered. Indeed, nothing at that moment could have been better, for it quieted the others, or else in a moment we had both been dead, or one of us worse. "Nothing could be better," I repeated; "but I will not stir from here, unless you make it a fair fight and give me fair play."

"Never fear, my fine gentleman! I'll give ye fair play enough, and a foot of good steel to the bargain! Here, you, Gowan," he added, turning to the tavern-keeper, who seemed to be surprisingly sober, of a sudden, too, "push away these tables, and you, my friends, if one of you does aught to interfere, I'll blow out his brains!" And he tapped a brace of pistols in his belt.

They obeyed him like lambs and set to work, push-ing the chairs and tables against the walls of the room, while two dragged the "jolly good fellow" by the shoulders under the bar. So much will a serious fight do to cool the wine-heated brains of men in such riotous times as these. For my part, I turned to the girl, to find her looking up at me with undisguised fright in her eyes.

"Keep close by the fire," said I quickly; "there is naught to fear" — though there was enough and to spare. For what might happen when I had settled this one, I could not tell.

A strange little smile passed over her face at what I had said, and then she answered:

"I will. But can you fight?"

Now, I do not know why it should, but it did, cut me to have such a question flung at me as I was on the point of going into a struggle that she alone had brought upon me. It might have seemed that she could think of some one but herself at such a mo-ment; but, as I have said, I do not understand the working of a woman's mind. So that, whatever I may have thought, I only said:

"We shall soon see, mistress, and for your sake, at least, I can but try."

She looked straight into my face again for a moment, and then moved over to the fireplace without a word.

"Now, then, sir, are you ready?" asked my man, and I answered by moving into the middle of the now cleared room. I liked it not in any way. The lights were bad. At best 't was but a fog, and a man cannot be blamed for wishing a good light to watch his enemy's eye. To one side of the room I could see five thievish-looking knaves standing together, and what I might expect of them at any moment could not be guessed.

Then, too, good swordsman as I was — and 't is no conceit that makes me say so, for I had had three years of work by day and night, and half a dozen before them of constant practice with my father, Captain Balfort, of the Indian wars — but, good swordsman as I might be, no fight is a surety, and I knew nothing of my antagonist, excepting that he was partly under the influence of liquor. If I fell, what might not become of the girl, what might not the papers in my boot mean to him, and those to whom he belonged. And it soon appeared to whom he belonged, for he crossed my sword at once, saying :

"And now for myself and for the king ! Watch out, you bastard, for I am the best of men to play with this tool!"

And, indeed, he was a master hand. I could tell at the first thrust that he was better than I, and had he been empty of liquor, this tale and my own life had ended there and then in that dirty room. He was inside my guard a dozen times in the first two minutes, as we circled round each other, playing constantly for the light of a single lantern that hung over the outer door.

Still, I was growing calmer, and had begun to gauge him better when he slipped over my thrust and ripped the shoulder of my coat with a sudden and a true stroke. Then, on the instant, I heard a stifled cry; and, glancing by his head, I saw the girl standing by the fire, leaning forward, her hands nervously clasped together at her throat, her hood down upon her shoulders, and a look of terror in her eyes.

"Ah," said the wretch, "my lady whimpers, does she? Fear not, I'll give her comfort when thou hast gone to hell."

'T was a spur that made me mad to think on, realising as I did that he had all but done for me that moment, and I went at him with every thrust and stroke I knew, beating his rapier till the room sang with the blows. But I could not touch him. He was a marvellous good hand, and no mistake; for he gave ground till I had him with his foot at the other wall, but not once did I get inside his guard.

"Keep your hounds in their place," I cried, between my fast-coming breath; for the men, whether from interest or with some foul design, had gathered closer to us.

"Stand off, you fools!" he cried in answer. "Do

ye not see I have him pinked already? Look ye at that — and that — and that!" And he broke away from the wall, and pressed me as I had never been pressed before, nor wish to be again. Once he touched me above the wrist, and I could feel the warm blood running down into my sword hand. This was no country lout, in good earnest, and I knew then that I had to do with some British officer without his uniform.

Another stifled cry came from the direction of the fireplace, sounding clear in the silent room, and a smile played over the man's mouth, as he muttered:

"Now one for the king!" And he drew a little away from me. I stood my ground and let him go. And as I took a breath or two to catch my wind, and brushed my left hand across my eyes to wipe away the sweat, I cried at him out of the bitterness of my heart:

"Damn you and your king, for villainous knaves! Come, are ye afraid, that ye draw away?"

Before I had well finished a look came into his eyes as he stooped, and then, with only the thought of saving myself from a thrust I did not know, I jumped to the right and thrust my sword straight out at him.

He had not counted on the quarts he had drunk, and the stooping posture must have affected his balance; for he lunged beyond his power to recover, and, as he half fell, half thrust by me, his blade went through the tail of my coat, and my own passed clean through the top of his left shoulder.

Down he went, carrying my sword with him, and a howl set up from the men.

"A foul blow! A foul blow!" they cried, and I had but time to pull my rapier away when they were upon me. The first to come caught my fist on his nose and rolled away with a groan of pain, but in an instant the others had me down. 'T was a wretched scramble of a fight, one against four, and I kicked and struck out and cursed them all for cowards, when on a sudden the officer's voice sounded high above the others, and with his one good arm and the tavern-keeper's assistance, he pulled the crowd off.

I jumped to my feet, dazed and nearly mad with anger, to receive a tap on my shoulder from the flat of his sword.

"Ye 've not finished with me, my friend! Have ye had enough?"

"I? You British spy! I had enough? I 'll send your poor soul to hell before I 've had enough!"

"Good!" said he. "Good! 'T is a proper spirit! But hell waits for others than me to-night;" and he was at me again with the blood running down the soaked sleeve of his left arm, that swung aimlessly at his side. The man was game beyond a doubt, and a strange respect for him crept over me, cooling my brain and giving me a sight of what I must do to save my own life.

Again he beat into my guard. Again he pushed me to the wall. But I was cooling down, and he could not stand the terrible strain. If I could but hold him off, his heavy drinking would sap his

strength before mine began to fail, and with that new
heart came to me, and I smiled on him as he worked
to touch me.

That, and the knowledge of his failing strength,
goaded him in a tender spot, and he lost his temper
and his easy air. I could hear him mutter a soft curse
now and then, and the cool smile was gone. Then I
tried again a dodging thrust that had met a wall of
cold steel earlier in the fight.

Waiting till he prepared a thrust of his own, I
parried with a too waving motion, and swung my
blade far out to the right. He saw the lost guard
at once, but saw too late how I drew in my arm and
turned the point at his breast. I dropped on both
knees as his rapier passed close by my head, and he
literally spitted himself on mine, falling heavily on
me without a sound.

Knowing what would come, I rolled him over, and,
jumping up, drew both pistols, and stood looking
about the room, which, through my blurred eyes,
showed me what seemed to be a hundred faces.

"The next will die sooner," I cried. "Which
shall it be? Which shall it be? Will ye not come,
none of you? Ah!"

And then, seeing some one rushing towards me, I
levelled the pistol straight at his head, raising my
eyebrows to get a clearer look, when, God help me,
I had like to have shot the girl!

"You are hurt," said she softly. "Where? Where
is it?" and, looking up at me with eyes that were
filled with tears, she took my right wrist and turned

back the sleeve. 'T was but a scratch, but his point
had touched a vein and let out a deal of blood, and
I saw her sway at the sight.

"Have a care," I said quickly; "they are coming;"
but she stirred not a step, and proceeded to wipe away
the blood from my arm. And then, growing cooler,
I saw the tavern-keeper warily stepping forward, bowing and apologising and keeping a sharp watch on my
two pistols.

"'T is over, sir. The men here will not break their
word" — a fine thing was their word, to be sure —
"but the gentleman is dying, sir."

For the first time I looked at him. He lay just as
I had rolled him over, but any one could see that he
breathed heavily still.

"Here, you, Jim," said Gowan. "You know
some'at of such things. Is he dead?"

The sallow-faced countryman stepped over and
straightened out the body, keeping a careful eye the
while on my pistol, as my companion swiftly and
gently bound her handkerchief above the cut and
stopped a part of the flow. Then she as gently
pushed me on to a stool by the table and stood with
her hand unconsciously resting on my shoulder as the
countryman ripped up the officer's jacket and bared the
wound.

"'T is beyond me," said he finally. "Ye can do
naught but wash it with clean water and wait."

"Take him into the other room here," said
Gowan, and three of them picked him up and carried
him into the inner part of the tavern.

CHAPTER III

I WAS unable to do aught. In truth, I could
not move, and so I sat there like a sick fool,
never stirring, except once to look up at my companion, and find her looking at me steadfastly; but
I could not say a word. And yet I could see the men
who had returned growing more and more confident,
as those who had carried the wounded officer away
talked in low tones to the others. But the minutes
gave me my wind and brought back some of my
nerve, and then they came on with set faces.

I stood up and grasped my pistols, but in that
moment the girl stepped forward with her head up
and as proud an air as ever chicken had against mail
coach.

"What do you wish?" she asked quietly.

"We want that man! He has killed one of us,
and —"

"One of you, you clowns?" I cried, taking her by
the shoulder and setting her aside. "He is no more
of you than I am!"

"Who are ye, then?" cried the spokesman. "And
what do ye here? We do not like the look of ye, and

ye shall go no further till ye settle with us and tell
us who ye may be."

It was no drunken crew that spoke now, and I knew
it. They had made up their minds, and I was too
weak to try to cope with four men. They seemed to
be natives hereabouts, and I must take my chances of
their being Colonials by sentiment as well as birth.
There was naught else to do.

"I am an American soldier," I said, "travelling
north alone, and you have no more to do with me
than with the river outside the door."

"I knew it!" cried the man, and the others began
to surround us. "Ye rebel bastard, ye 've struck
the wrong gang! Travelling alone, eh? And what
is this baggage here with ye?"

"She?" said I, stumped again. "Why, she —"

"I am his sweetheart," said the girl, stepping before
me again. Then she went on in an earnest way that
finally became plaintive: "We have run away to be
married. Will you not help us to make merry?
We 've but just escaped from New York. Indeed,
we have! You can see our coach broken down in
the road not a hundred yards from here — you can,
indeed, sirs!"

Her breath was coming fast, but she went on with
excited earnestness that caught the men: "Our coach
boys will be here shortly with the horses. You can
see the coach if you will but go down the road! He
does not tell the truth! He is no rebel! 'T is not so,
good sirs! Will you not drink a bumper to the king
and to our honeymoon?"

I could not say a word. I could do naught but stare
open-mouthed at her, for, with the skill of intuition,
she had hit the one point — would they not drink a
bumper to us — *would* they? The one thing to win
them over! Then I caught her arm. What was she
doing? 'T was a foolish and a futile plan.

"See, sirs, you see he tries to make me deny it!
But I will not. You would not injure a good soldier
of his majesty, would you? And you will drink to
our health and happiness. Mr. Landlord, will you
not fill us up mugs of ale to drink the toast?" And
she stepped back, and took my arm with a hand that
shook like a leaf, though her eyes never wavered
from the men she addressed.

"By God! 'T is a brave wench," cried one of the
men. "And a health it shall be!"

"Stay," said another, a huge clout, who was no
more a Britisher than I. "I do not believe it! He
called our friend in there a British spy. Dost know
that?"

"But I say she shall have the health," cried the
other. "Jack Purdy, ye have no soul in ye! Can
ye not see the girl tells the truth?"

"Aye, look at him," said a third; "he's a shamefaced bridegroom!"

"We'll do it in shape," said the first. "Here
you, Gowan" — to the landlord — "tell Jim Marvin
to come in here. Now, mistress, to you and your
happiness!"

"To you!" chorused the crowd. And we two
stood there, the shaking arm in mine, the brave eyes

smiling a forced smile, but looking the men in the face, as she raised the filthy pewter to her lips and touched the ale. The devil himself could not make me drink, till I bethought me of another toast, and, turning to her, drained the cup without a word.

The sombre individual, who it appeared was Marvin, now entered; and I watched them confer with him. A laugh broke from his tipsy lips, and he muttered: "'T would be a good close! Here am I saving one man's life, and now paving the way for the making of others." And still we two stood there, waiting, neither looking nor speaking to the other.

"So it shall be!" cried the big one in a moment, and instinctively I clutched a pistol as they all moved over towards the fireplace near us.

"You say ye 've just run away to be married, do you?" asked the man.

She nodded.

"Very well, then, we 'll have the ceremony here and now. Here 's Marvin, as good at marrying as at curing dead men, and we 'll have the ceremony and celebrate the wedding this night, damned if we don't, eh, boys?" Another chorus of assent greeted this. But I found my tongue at last.

"That you shall not," said I firmly.

"Then string him up for a rebel, and we 'll take good care of the girl!" cried one. I broke away from my companion and levelled two muzzles at the nearest fellow.

"The first to move is dead," said I, hopeless though I knew it was.

"Tut, man, we'll punch you full of holes, if you talk like that," said Marvin, smiling with the assurance of five to one. "And, then, why should you not join us? What harm to be married now, if you have run away to be? And will you have all the fun to yourself? Nay, nay," he went on in his nasal tone. "You've broken up our evening now, and ye'll break your own neck or help us to finish it in our own way. Gowan! Hey, Gowan! Where is the man? Here," he added, as the tavern-keeper stuck his nose through the door, "bring us a Bible."

The door swung wide open.

"A Bible!" cried the astounded man.

"Aye, a Bible."

"And what, think ye, would I be doing with a Bible?"

"God knows," said the other. "Little enough. But we do not need one. Come, man" — turning to me — "stand there."

I turned to the girl, and she looked up at me. I read in her face what she saw in mine. We must go through with the thing, or in half an hour she would be at the mercy of these outlaws.

"Why not, my friends?" she said, turning to them. "I cannot be married too soon. Else why should I have run away from home?"

After all, the man was no minister, and a forced affair like this could mean nothing. And so there, in the reeking room, with one man in a stupor and with five as wicked specimens of humanity as it had ever been my lot to meet, the drunken Marvin married us in the early morning hours. How the wretch knew aught of the marriage service I could not then tell. But he did, and we agreed by nods — only speaking when forced to — to cleave to each other in sickness and in health, in good fortune and in bad, till death should us part.

When he came to ask my name, I hesitated, and was about to give another, and then — curse me for a careless beast — the man called Purdy spoke up, reading from the rim of my hat: "Balfort."

And so I gave my name.

"Mistress," said Marvin, "your name now."

"Deborah Philipse," she said, beneath her breath, and then repeated a part of what he dictated, though her arm grew heavier and heavier in mine till my wounded wrist throbbed with pain.

I thought then it was over, but he must needs get paper and ink, and write out a blurred and rambling certificate that Merton Balfort and Deborah Philipse were married the 19th day of September, 1780, by James Marvin, minister of the gospel; whereupon those looking on roared with laughter at him and his solemnity, and most of all at his signature that covered half the page. When he had signed, Purdy cried out:

"Now, a toast to the bride!" and we filled again, and they drank and I tasted.

But Marvin stood up, keeping his balance as best he could, and droned out in mock solemnity:

"Gentlemen, you forget. The minister has not had his fee."

Then, turning to me, he said in a wheedling tone, with a horse-pistol pointing at me from his right hand, "You would not forget the man of God that made you the possessor of such as this?"

Indeed, I had not seen it until that moment, nor had it occurred to me till then that I had on my first night in this country fallen in with a gang of Skinners. It was clear enough now, and the amusement they were to have, and were having, while robbing me was of their own devilish making.

"Let me pay the fee," said the girl eagerly, and, drawing out a silken purse, she took from it half a dozen gold pieces — enough for forty weddings — and handed them to Marvin, adding, "I thank you, sir."

I could have cried with rage at this last, the simplicity of the girl's vision, coupled with her infinite skill in turning the whole episode from a fight into a peaceful, or rather harmless, robbery!

Marvin held the pieces in his hand, and made a wry face as he leered at her.

"'T is but a small sum for so great a service, Mistress Balfort!"

"Why — " said she, with a vacant stare, and then looked at me. Something must have shown on my face; for, with a sudden catching of her hand at her throat and a falling of her smiling mask, she handed him the purse and turned away.

Marvin counted out the pieces with slow precision, and then turned to his gang.

"This is but a paltry pair after all," said he. "And

never have I had so small a marriage fee. Can you not help your lady wife out, good sir?" — addressing me.

An uncontrollable movement that I made drew four long barrels on my head not five feet away, and with a groan I threw him my wallet.

It held a goodly sum, and I prayed that they might forget to search me, for what else I had lay with my despatches in my boots. But a savage grunt from the other side of the room saved us. Every eye turned towards the sound, and we saw the "jolly good fellow" wriggle and sit up. He was dressed like my opponent, and I was watching him as he struggled to his feet, when a spasmodic grasp clutched my arm. I turned to see Mistress Philipse's face close up to mine and abject terror written on every feature.

"That man! That man!" gasped she. "Save me from him, in God's name!" And — whether because this was the last straw, or because of some new and greater danger from this last addition to our company, I know not — she leaned against me and would have fallen had I not picked her up and carried her into the other part of the tavern.

The door opened into a hall, and from that I turned into the first room, which, as often in such houses, was a bedroom; there I laid her on the bed and took off her soaked shoes. She lay quiet, and I seized the chance to seek the landlord. He was not far, for I found him standing looking at me as I came into the dark hall.

"Gowan," said I, "you have as villainous a lot

here as ever I saw, but if you be the man I think you, you will get me out of this place."

"What can I do with them, sir? They own the house now. 'T will be a godsend if they do not burn it about our ears!"

"Go back down the road and find the coach. You'll get a hundred times the pay there for what I want you to do."

"I'll do what I can," he muttered.

"Give me another horse and a woman's saddle, if you have it."

"I have none but an old man's saddle."

"You'll find two horses hitched to the coach. Keep them." For, if the men had not taken them, they must still be there. The men, I knew, would be gone by this.

"I cannot get the horse for ye just now," he muttered, standing first on one foot and then on the other.

"Come with me, then," said I, and we went back to the main room. 'T was a ticklish job, but we did it. They were at their jolly good fellow again — now he sat on a stool with his head in his hands — and they hailed me as an old friend. I must needs drink with them and sing a snatch. But we put a keg on the table and stole out, leaving them fighting for the first draught of it.

We found the coach, but, as I feared, neither men nor horses. Still, there was that in the travelling box which more than satisfied Gowan, and we soon had another horse saddled standing with Roger ready in a shed just above the tavern. On getting again into the back room by a rear door, I found the girl sitting up on the bed. She clung to me, and cried out in a smothered voice:

"That man! That man! Is there another with him? There must be! They are always together!"

"There's no other here, madam. Do but keep quiet, and all will be well."

"We must get away," she begged again.

"You could not ride now, and an hour hence the men will be beyond the power to follow us. Hark — they are at it again;" and, indeed, only the dead could fail to hear them.

I got her to lie down again, and went and sat outside the door, till she cried out that I was leaving her to them. And so I came and sat by the bed, and, as I am a sinner, nothing would do but she must have her little hand in mine. 'T was a strange thing for Merton Balfort. And once I turned, when I dared, to look at her, and saw her asleep with her head lying on the pillow, still in its frame of wonderful wavy hair.

CHAPTER IV

AS TO THE MOODS OF A MAIDEN

WE had been walking the horses slowly a good hour northward, for I had no choice but to get on with my journey. The rain had stopped, and the first light of a September day began to show up over the high land to the eastward. Not a word had we said since getting well started. I, for one, had more to think than talk on, and the girl was too wearied to do more than sit in her ungainly saddle, while I led her wretched nag.

Heaven knows, I am no poet, and never was; but the break of that day was a beautiful thing to see. All the earth was wet and glistening on the barest excuse for light. The trees all but met over our heads, with now and then an open bit of country, and here and there a sight of the big river. And all the little noises of the morning — the insects, the birds — kept up a singing and a wheezing and a droning that would make the heart bound within you.

Then would come a little more light, and the trees would separate and stand up of themselves, and you could tell houses from sand banks. And from a strange and ghostly whiteness there came a big red glow, like a sunset, but still never was that light at setting sun. Here and there was a red-tipped bough, while the big rocks across the stream burned with the colour. Then I watched the colour go by and the first white light of the sun pitch against the cliffs, catch the trees above us, and then come dropping around us on the wet turf and the red mud at our feet. And another clear day was come out of as filthy a night as one could guess at.

" 'T is a very fine day," said a strange voice at my side.

I turned in my saddle in wonder, and found her looking up at the trees overhead and the sky through them, and then turned back in my saddle and said not a word. What might be her ladyship's next mood? As for myself, I was too worn out, too uncertain as to my next move, to see aught in the situation but desperate outlook and small chance of my mission finishing that day or week.

So the noisy silence of the wood began again.

" You have not the manners of his majesty's court, sir," said she blandly.

" I have never had occasion to be there, mistress," I answered, with some meaning to my tone.

" No? " said she, and studied the green leaves about her for a space. " 'T is a wretched thing," she added, after a bit.

" What, the court? "

" Nay, the want of the manners."

"Perhaps you would prefer to return to the others;" and then I stuck a spur into old Roger and cursed myself for a fool.

3

She said not a word for a moment, and then:

"A courtly response, indeed. Where were you bred, sir?"

"In what, God be thanked, is a free country, mistress. The town of Boston, in Massachusetts colony."

"Oh! I have heard tell of it. A little wandering town, where men pray for eight days in the week, and a woman may wear only black and never raise her eyes from the buckle of her slipper."

"'T is a town of great men and big hearts, Mistress Philipse. And 't is not for even a British butterfly to demean it."

"Am I, I wonder, Mistress Philipse?" said she, looking at me with a glint in her eye. "Or —"

"I do not know, madam. That was the name you took but a few hours since." She had a look in her face that for the life of me I could not read. Was it a bursting desire to laugh, or a vixen's love of teasing?

"Or, am I Mistress — Mistress — Balfort, is it?"

"If you were so indeed, you should not speak thus of the Cradle of Liberty."

"Ah, indeed! And would you tell me who should prevent it?"

"That I will, mistress. No other than your husband."

"Ah, indeed!" said she again. "I see that you have lived much in the company of women and know them full well, Captain Balfort."

"Lieutenant Balfort, at your service, mistress."

"You should be a captain, sir," said she, looking

up through the trees. "You bore yourself as such not many hours since."

The change of tone was so quick that for some unknown reason I grew red with shame, and asked seriously enough:

"Will you tell me why you should go through a bad scene as brave as any — any soldier, and then faint at sight of a drunken man?"

"Ah, do not speak of him!" cried she, turning a face that on a sudden had a bit of that terror in it again. And then, looking back on the road, " Think you they may follow us?"

"Nay, mistress," I answered. "Not one of them could stand."

"Then why will you bring me back to that tavern, when I am tired and would talk of other things?"

" 'T was a thoughtless query, and I ask your forgiveness," said I, riding closer to her, for I thought she would sway off the nag's back.

But her eye grew bright again on a sudden.

"Do not fear, sir," said she, with her chin in the air. "I am no chicken-hearted maid. I do not require the support of an arm — not even when that arm belongs to a husband."

"Mistress Philipse," said I earnestly, resting a hand on her horse's mane, "you have twice referred to a part of last night's performance with the scorn that, God knows, you no doubt feel. But you are in the wrong to give it any credence, except as the brave act of a brave woman, who saved by her ready wit her companion from sure death and herself from worse.

Do you, perchance, think that that companion places any other significance upon it?"

She turned her head away and looked down at the wet ferns by the roadside for a moment without reply, and then, looking me in the face, answered:

"'T is a foolish question, Lieutenant, and you know it as well as I. Therefore will I not answer it."

Why it should be so I cannot tell, but the certainty that I saw in her face of the whole event's absurdity gave me a sinking within myself that turned me back in my saddle and put out the brightness of the morning.

So again we rode on for a space.

"You do not ask me why I am in this dreadful country alone and at such a time," said she firmly.

"No, mistress, I do not. But I would ask another question, if you should choose to permit it."

"And what may it be?"

"No other than where are you going?"

For a moment she looked at me with that glint in her eye, and then burst into as merry a fit of laughter as it has been my lot to hear. I looked at her in amazement, not unmixed with irritation, and off she went in another ripple, till I had nigh broken forth into more remarks that would doubtless have called down other sarcasms.

"'T is no doubt most ludicrous," said I, at length, somewhat bitterly, "but I have not yet discovered that side of it and cannot join your humour."

"Oh, can you not, indeed?" she laughed. "Could you but look on your own face at this moment, you 'd discover soon enough."

"I do not see what my face, ludicrous as it may be, has in common with the end of your journey."

"Why, I am travelling with my — "

I turned quickly upon her, and she stopped and flushed as red as the morning sun but a couple of hours ago.

"I — I am going to a place just above here," she stammered with a sober face. "And I would tell you, sir, in order that you may not misjudge me, that I have run away from home, because — "

"Because — ?" said I, in spite of myself, for I should have asked hours ago had I dared.

"Because I chose to," she answered, and then, turning two eyes on me that boded no good in them to those who crossed her, she went on, sitting straight up in the old saddle; "because they will learn some day that I will do what I see fit to do, and will not do what neither God nor man should expect of me!"

Who is it, I wonder, that says something of the lucidity of a woman's mind? I knew no more why she had left her home, if she had one, than I did before her reply, but I would no more have asked at that moment for definite information than I would have banged my head against yonder big maple by the roadside. So I held my peace, and she sat there astride her horse with her head up and the glance of a queen.

She was going to some place about here. Then I could get on my way and attend to my mission. That was what I wanted, no doubt. It would be a lucky thing for me to get my mind on my work and carry it through. I was, of course, pleased at this, and a load was lifted from my shoulders.

"Why do you look so glum?" said she. "Do you perhaps take their side?"

"God forbid, mistress!" said I. 'They' might go to Limbo before I would stretch out a hand to help them. "I was thinking of other matters."

"Oh, were you, indeed? I suppose that you are so accustomed to riding about the earth with women that their conversation wearies you."

I lifted my hand to interrupt her, but she went rushing on:

"And I would ask you a question, too, Mr. Balfort. Will you give me that paper?"

"That paper?" said I, in amazement.

"Yes, sir. That paper which you have in your pocket, and which I signed last night;" and I saw a bit of colour go slowly over her face and into her hair, as she looked at me, and then at Roger's nose, and then back at me.

"Why, I think — I fear it is lost," I muttered.

"Do not lie to me, sir! 'T is in your pocket. I saw you put it there when 't was signed."

And so I drew the scrawled slip from my pocket and handed it to her, as she had bid. She took it slowly and looked at it for a moment as the horses walked on quietly, and then she put it between the lacings of her bodice, and the colour ran over her face again, like the little haze that passes across the moon of a windy night.

"Look!" said she suddenly. "We are coming to a village. See the houses. I think I will walk a bit."

I got down; and she, looking at me with a little
smile, placed her two hands on my shoulders and let
me lift her out of the ungainly saddle and set her on
the ground, wondering the while how so much temper and changeableness could possibly be contained
in such a little body, for she could not have weighed
eight stone. As I threw the reins of the two horses
over my arm and started along the only partly dried
ruts by her side, she laughed that little laugh again:

"Of what do you suppose I am thinking, Mr.
Balfort?"

"Heaven forbid that I should pretend to guess,
madam."

"I am thinking," she answered, and laughed again
—"I am thinking that if I do not have something
to eat this minute, I shall die."

"The devil take me for a careless lout," I cried,
and forthwith drew out from my pocket a dirty bit
of paper—the only thing I could find at the tavern
—and opened out a moderately clean piece of bread
and a slice or two of ham. She looked up at me in
surprise, and impulsively held out her hand.

"You are a good, thoughtful man, after all!"

And I, I, this same Balfort—what the fiend had
gotten into my crop this day?—I raised it, and put
my lips to the little knuckles.

"Aha, sir," cried she with a twinkle in her eye,
"Boston is not so far from his majesty's court as I
have been led to infer!" I dropped the hand as if
it had been a hot cake, and turned to the horses, cursing myself for an ass.

Then she sat down by the roadside on a rock and proceeded to eat the bread and ham with as healthy an appetite as if she had just come from a canter across the meadows on her favourite mare. After a bit we searched about between the road and the river, and at last came upon a pretty spring, glittering in the sunshine, and I showed her how to lie at full length and drink from the pool itself.

So we walked on into the village, through it, and on out into the country again. She had refused to rest, as I suggested, in one of the houses, giving no reason except that she did not care to, and since passing the last one we had walked on in silence, until, without warning or introduction, she suddenly turned to me and said:

"You know that I have left my father's house in the city."

"Yes," I answered, not venturing too many opinions.

"You know, too, that you are in my eyes a rebel."

"Yes."

"A treasonable person, who should by rights be hanged."

"Yes."

"A very dangerous person, who breaks the king's laws, and must not be recognised or tolerated for an instant."

"Yes."

"Then, sir, when we reach the gate of that large house which you see yonder, get you gone at once, if you have any regard for me."

"Any regard for *you?*" I asked in astonishment.

"Why, yes."

"Why 'yes'?"

"Because, sir, I do not care to witness a hanging of any kind, whether of rebels or king's law breakers, or dangerous persons — or — or — near relatives."

I looked at her and saw her face as serious as it had yet been.

"That is the house of a Tory — a Royalist — and you stop there?"

"I do," she answered, looking off towards it.

"Do you know of the great danger of such a house in this neutral country, open to all the marauders that prowl about — of such men as we saw last night?"

"I do perfectly. That is why the people have left it."

"And you are going there alone?"

"Except for the servants."

"And who will hang me, if it please your ladyship to answer?"

"I shall be obliged to order the servants to serve their king."

I laughed for the very absurdity of it.

"Mistress Philipse, if you are indeed to stop here, I shall conduct you to the house and see that you are properly cared for."

"You will do nothing of the kind, sir."

"But think you that I fear your servants, or your king's edicts?"

"No, but you do me and mine."

"Do you think so, indeed?" said I, a little nettled.

"Yes, because I will beg you to go on," she said,

turning quickly to me and putting her hand on my arm, looking up into my face with an earnest appeal in her eyes; "because I am quite safe, because I — I — you have been a true gentleman this night and day, and because I would not have you do aught to make me think otherwise of you." The beautiful eyes were filling with tears as she went on. "Because I have perhaps done a foolish thing, and am quite safe now, and would not do other foolish things, and because — because you are too kind not to do what I ask;" and she was through the gate and gone up the walk to the house before I could speak.

I stood watching her running on, powerless to follow, and, as she reached the corner of the house, she turned back and waved her hand to me once — and then she was gone.

Slowly I tied the old nag to the gate-post. Slowly I mounted Roger and headed the good horse up the road, keeping my eyes the while upon the corner of the house around which the little figure in its hood and cape had disappeared. And so I sat across Roger until the trees shut out the view.

CHAPTER V

STRANGE — so strange I could not get over
it — that the last twenty-four hours had set
the world wagging another way for me.
There was Fanny Jaekel up in Boston, whom I had
known so many years, whom I 'd have sworn even
now was of the best a man might ever hope or wish
to call his own. And had I, perhaps, thought to do
so some day?

There 's but little good in denying what we know
to be so, and 't is quite true that I had thought again
and again of dear little Fanny watching for me from
a certain window some day when I came homeward,
and giving me the doings of her sex at supper, as I
gave her those of mine in exchange.

Will not man or boy of any age do the same thing
a hundred times in as many months? But Fanny
seemed to have been there longest, oftenest. Yet had
I never so much as suspected in all this what was
tearing through my mind now after as uncanny a
night as a man might dread to be repeated.

There stood Fanny's little white face against every
tree as we — Roger and I — trudged on; and somewhere behind it, shining through it, looking strangely

at me, another that I had seen but part of a day —
angry, proud, kind, humorous, anything but sweet, as
it stared at me with the looks of so many different
Fannies and all her friends that I'd ever known swallowed up in something new. I could have dropped
off Roger and kicked myself for a light-headed fool
to think such a twist could come to me and switch
my mind around to so different a view.

And I was like to have been off the horse, at any
rate, just then, for through the string of my thoughts
rang out clear on the morning air the loud "ping"
of a rifle, just ahead, but so near that Roger got away
across the road a little quicker than I. Standing so
an instant, I caught the unmistakable sounds of a
combat — curses, blows, cries, and the ring of steel;
and without thinking overmuch, I put the horse to
his run, and covered the short space to a turn where
a thicket of shrubs shut out the stretch of the road.

As we turned the corner, there in the middle of the
highway stood four men, three of them ragged, one
of huge stature and better dressed, the latter talking
and laughing with rasping sarcasm as the other three
set on him, but ever keeping them away with his long
sword. I was scarce twenty yards from them, and
so fetched the lead from my pistol into the side of
one, and caught a second on the head with the weapon
itself, as Roger flew past the group. The surprise
was equal for all five of us, but the big one did not
appear disturbed in the least. As I pulled up and
turned, I heard him cry out:

"Now! Now, my ragged son of the woods, 't is

evener! Let me cut thy beautiful pate open! So!
So again! Ho! Here! Stop, you left-handed patriot! Oh, 't is a shame! 'T is a shame!" And he
was off in among the trees after the third of the
gang.

One was dead for sure, and lay there in the mud.
But the other got up to a sitting posture, rubbing the
side of his head, as I came over him; and he gazed
up at me with a dazed surprise in his countenance
so comical to look upon that I roared with laughter,
to be interrupted by a loud, mocking voice:

"Nay, 't is no laughing matter, sir. Here have you
caused me to lose a gentleman of great value by your
sudden interruption!"

"I?" cried the most astonished of all now, "I?
My interruption?"

"Of a surety," said the giant, with a laughing
face, and he grasped my hand warmly. "Here was
I getting some little morning exercise with my three
friends, and you must break in and —"

"I beg your pardon, sir," said I, bowing low. "I
fancied you had miscalculated the courtesy of these
same friends."

"And," continued he — "and commit the strange
breach in time of war of saving me from furnishing
a delicate meal to my friends over there on the trees.
But which tree did ye drop from yourself?"

"No such interesting feature in it," said I; "the
road and the abrupt curve made the whole thing appear over sudden."

"My devoirs to the abrupt curve," said the young

man with mock courtesy, lifting his cap to the white
highway. "And now, sir, whoever ye may chance
to be, the chance is so good for me that I would
shake you by the hand, and thank you for your saving of my worthless neck, and say to you that when
John Acton can do aught for you — why, by the
Lord, call on him and try him!"

And he held out his enormous hand with a frank-
ness that I had done well to have trusted.

But I had been too close to failing in my mission
more than once in the last twenty-four hours, and
too close to losing my own head to try any more ex-
periences with strangers; and I, therefore, shook him
by the hand, telling him the whole thing was naught
to speak of again, and went no further. But as he
asked me to accompany him to a hollow off the road
where ran a brook, that he might wash the blood
from his face and hair, I could see that I had hurt
him by lacking in the confidence he showed.

Little was said as he knelt by the stream, till I
caught the sound of horses' feet, and looked up to
see a troop of uniformed men coming from the north
over a steep hill. As they clattered down the slope,
I made up my mind that 't was approaching the time
when I should leave.

As he raised his head at the sound, he quickly took
me by the arm and stepped across the brook into the
shrubbery.

" 'T is a safe thing to avoid two skirmishes in the
same hour," said he with a jovial laugh; and I
agreed with him in more ways than one. Then:

"Do you stay here a bit, while I find out who they may be," for the troop had pulled up where the stream crossed the road.

It was my chance now, if ever, and with the light step I had learned from my father's lessons, got by hard years in the Indian wars — a step that never broke a twig nor rustled a leaf unnecessarily — I was away in a moment, making for the direction of the river bank in the hope of getting to the other side; for, in good earnest, this was too populous a country for me to move in just now.

As I got away, I heard a hail from the big lungs of Mr. John Acton, but it only added to my speed, and, by the best chance that for once turned my way, I made the river bank, paid a fellow near by to ferry me across, and got into the woods on the other side. So, keeping close by the road, but avoiding it whenever I gathered that some one was approaching, I moved along towards Haverstraw.

One would have said the whole world walked abroad that day, for I met one after another; till, the sense of caution growing stronger in me for what I had been through, I stepped towards the river bank into the thick forest, and lay me down to wait for darkness. In good truth, what with the want of food and the work of the past night, I needed rest badly, and my wandering thoughts, that strayed back to a certain tavern and its strangely fair occupant, must soon have been overruled by honest sleep, for when I sat up again, with the sense of something occurring, or about to occur, near by, darkness had settled over the land for several hours.

It has ever been a peculiar quality of mine to wake fully at once, and I had made no movement when there came in on my mind, less through the eyes than the ears, that there, in the moonlit woods, walked some one. A turn of the head showed me the figure of a man striding up and down, his hands clasped behind his back, his head bent forward, but each moment nervously lifted, as if expecting to hear some sound near by.

"An officer," said I to myself, for the square shoulders, the straight figure, and the unknown something in the carriage of a man accustomed to military precision were visible in every movement of the figure. I could not trust myself to move, for he passed constantly within a few feet of the spot where I lay, only separated from me by the great elm whose roots had served me for a pillow.

"An officer, and no mistake," went on my musings, "and here in the woods at night, by the river, waiting, it would seem, for some one. Can it be that he grows impatient? He moves towards the stream. No." My musings were cut short by the unmistakable sound of oars regularly striking the tholepins of a boat. The noise drew near, and the boat must have stopped close by, for in a moment a man—nay, two— appeared, and one at least was an officer as well, for beneath his long coat dangled the point of a scabbard. The one who waited retreated to my tree, and stood not five feet away in a deep shadow, while the other two came up the bank into the little open glade.

Gradually it dawned upon me that I was, by some

strange freak of chance, become the spectator in the gallery, so to speak, of a theatre. What the spectacle should be, I knew not; but a strong, perhaps natural, feeling led me to watch with peculiar eagerness for what was about to take place.

There was not long to wait; for the older man stepped guardedly from the shadows near me, and, on the moment, one of the new arrivals said in a low tone:

"Is that you, General?"

"It is I," said the deep tones of the elderly officer.

"This is Mr. Anderson — Mr. John Anderson, whom you expect."

"There is none other with you?"

"None," answered the first speaker. "Except the two boatmen below, and they be out of earshot." Then he who seemed to be master of ceremonies in this strange midnight drama continued: "Mr. Anderson, this is Mr. Gustavus, of whom we have spoken."

Thereupon went over me a cold sweat, for there could be no mistake — the third party to this drama spoke with a clear, strong voice in the unmistakable accents of an Englishman:

"I am, then, in the presence of Mr. Gustavus?"

"You are," replied that person. "There is no reason for raising our voices. I have the honour, then, of addressing Mr. John Anderson."

"The same."

What had an Englishman to do here, within, or nearly within, American lines? And what meant this meeting? Here were the voices and figures of officers!

4

No country louts were thus getting together in the midst of the woods. The tones, too, were of a character with the time and place. Those of him called Anderson were distant and of no very forbearing nature. Those of the older man came from one who was in haste.

"I understand, sir," said Mr. Anderson, "that you are the person who has made certain communications touching the fortifications at West Point."

"Yes," answered Mr. Gustavus.

"I am given to understand further," went on the English voice, "that there has arisen some question as to the sincerity of both parties, especially as regards Sir Henry Clinton."

"Yes," came the answer again.

Sir Henry Clinton! In spite of myself, I sat up, as if forced by a spring, and the third member of this strange trio must have taken the rustle of the leaves to be the night wind, for he turned and certainly heard the sound. Sir Henry Clinton! Sir Henry Clinton!

"I am here, sir, to prove my chief's sincerity," the English voice was saying, as the spectator in this theatre gathered his scattered wits. "I am here in reply to a note from Mr. Gustavus, which says that he will hand to Mr. Anderson the plans of the fortress at West Point, together with a list of the guns, as a sign of his good faith and sincerity and as a first step in the arrangements to be consummated. Am I correct?"

"So I understand, sir," replied the elderly officer quickly.

MAJOR JOHN ANDRE,

Adjutant General to his Majesty's Forces in North
under the Command of Sir Henry Clinton

"I have the *honour,* then, of addressing General Benedict Arnold?"

"Yes; and I?"

"Of addressing Major John André, of Clinton's staff — but what is that?"

"'T is the wind in the leaves," answered the master of ceremonies. "I heard it but now;" and, by the grace of chance, the wind did indeed at that moment rustle among the foliage on all sides. Otherwise, my spasmodic movement must have discovered me then and there.

What followed will never be clear to me, for my mind became on the instant so crazed with the idea that was growing on me moment by moment, that I can but recall a certain sense of moonlight and woods, with three tall figures standing in a bit of open swale, talking as if for my benefit, while I lay there in a dream. Yet do I remember the so-called Gustavus saying:

"May I ask what is your plan for the taking of the fortifications?"

"'T is that on the 28th the attack should be made by falling quickly on the southern outposts, and that you, expecting us, should have made the way clear by leaving pickets widely separated, by having the garrison unprepared, and by showing me on the plans the exact position of the guns and the spot where we may enter."

Again comes a vacancy in my mind till I heard:

"As to my requirements. The letters do not speak as clearly of them as I could wish."

"All will be as you require — personal protection, the stated amount, and a command for yourself," replied the man called André.

"Besides the further details?"

"Besides the further details."

"It will only be necessary for you to meet me, then, on the 25th, when I shall deliver over the plans —"

An exclamation broke from André.

"You have no plans with you, then?" said he in a stern voice.

"'T was unsafe to bring them to a first meeting. The description of arrangements and the strength of the approaches were sent you a week ago."

"Those are now in my chief's hands, but 't is necessary that we have the complete plans."

"They will be ready on the 25th."

"Where is Washington?" asked André suddenly. His tone, the figure looming in the half light, both spoke of impatience and dissatisfaction.

"At Fishkill."

"And that is —"

"On the other bank, above my house, which stands opposite the fortress."

I could do naught but lie back and gaze in silence at the branches overhead, with the indescribable weight of something terrible on my mind, even as in boyhood I had often lain quiet in my bed at home when wakened suddenly from a wild dream, half in belief that 't was true, half conscious that indeed such things could not be. How long it may have been I could no more tell than I can describe the feelings that gov-

erned me, but certain it is that I suddenly became a-
ware of a movement on the part of the three towards
the boat. Then some discussion arose; I still lay flat
upon my back, gazing upward, but loud and angry
words came to me, and the figures of the three returned.

" 'T is a strange mischance, but we must not excite
them," the voice of Arnold was saying. "Do you,
Squire Smith, go with them to Haverstraw, and Major
André and I will walk to your house. I can give him
the papers there."

And in an instant they were gone.

So I lay a space. How long? The good God only
knows! But of a sudden the reaction took me, and
I started up with but one idea raging through my
head. To get to Fishkill! To give the story to my
great chief! To see him catch the traitor before the
28th could come upon us!

How 't was done no one can tell, least of all myself.
But cross the river again I did, and then, without head
or planning, I began to run upstream until I should
find a house, or a horse, or any one or thing that
might help me to get on the faster. It may have been
an hour, or two, or more. I cannot tell. Always I
ran on and on. My ears sang loudly, and the breath
had gone from me long ago.

Good runner and strong man as I was, I could not
tell from step to step how 't was that I got on. In
the rutted road and the slippery mud I fell again and
again; my hat and sword were gone long since. As
I look back on it now, it must have been close upon

a lunatic that plunged on northward through that night.

There came an end, however; one that was most sudden and unexpected. For I caught a cry, just as I saw a huge figure loom up ahead in the mist, of "Who goes there?" and saw the long line of a rifle go up to a shoulder.

'T was no time for parleying, and on the instant I cried out to let me pass, and discharged my pistol straight before me. There came but one sound — too loud for a pistol — and a hot streak passed along my scalp and through my hair.

"Stand away!" cried I.

"Phat 's that?" cried a voice. "Give the counter-sign!"

"I do not know it!" cried I, doggedly.

"I t'ought not!" came the rich brogue.

"I must see General Washington at once!" I cried, the tears of exhaustion and disappointment running down my face.

"Ho! ye 'll see him soon enough, me frind — phat the divil are ye, though?" he added, as a lantern was brought by some others, who ran up. "For the love o' Gawd! phat lunatic is it?" he cried, when he caught a glimpse of my face and clothes.

"Let me by, man! Who are you? Where am I?"

"Ye 're all right, me lad," laughed the sentinel; "ye 're me prisoner, and ye 're jist wan foot inside the Tiller's P'int picket line, goin' north!"

CHAPTER VI

IN WHICH A PRISONER IS TRIED AND HIS JAILER ESCAPES

WITH only a dim idea of what I went through the rest of that night, I can recall moving under escort to an old farm building, which appeared to serve the purpose of a guard-house, and, after a short examination, being committed to a back room with but one window, and that barred. For the few remaining hours before I was called out to the examining officer, I heard the steady tread of a sentinel outside my door. Sleep was gone from me, and like as not the rest I had had in the woods saved me from complete exhaustion.

Up and down the room I went hour by hour, trying to cool myself down and to form some plan for getting away and giving information to the high authority who alone could be told such news. But nothing came of it. Indeed, I was far too crazed with the experience I had had to gather my poor wits, except in so far as I decided finally to explain frankly who I was to the commanding officer of the troops stationed here at Verplancks. I knew Colonel Livingstone to be a fine soldier and a gentleman. My two letters had been taken from me as soon as I was brought in, but I had no fears for anything except my ability to come up with the Commander-in-Chief and get speech with him.

It was in the midst of this continual tramping up and down the room that I was interrupted by the entrance of a sergeant, who bade me follow him. We passed along a narrow hall, and stood at a half opened door, waiting to be called, as I supposed. Within the room could be heard the voice of an officer making examinations, but as I leaned wearily against the door-post I gradually became aware of two or three men talking in low voices on the other side of the door.

" Perchance 't was indeed the man, Rob, though, upon my soul, I hope not. For he did me as great a service as man can do." I started involuntarily. It was certainly the big voice of my friend John Acton of the morning before; and, while I listened, the turning of my thoughts to him led them, for the first time since that strange meeting in the woods, back to the old house at Gowan's Ferry and to her who had taken such a hold upon me; so that at first the words seemed to carry little meaning to my mind.

" Heaven bring it that 't is indeed your man, John. For I have followed the fellow up and down this country now for two weeks, till the pursuit of him and the desire to come up with him have grown to a strange fascination." This other voice was clear, cool, and penetrating, and came of a different character from such as one saw day by day among officers and men in the rank and file of the Continental army. 'T was no English accented voice, but it showed a great degree of cultivation.

"What bearing and clothes had he? Though the clothes might be changed," he added. "But I have seen that fiend again and again, always riding, always with a great cape, always at night."

"True, lad," said the other; "he did, indeed, wear a great cape, and he rode down from the heavens at full speed to my rescue."

"And then disappeared?"

"Aye, like the smoke from a gun — pouf! and he was gone."

"And some ten miles this side of Gowan's Ferry," the first voice said musingly; "'t was thereabouts I've come upon him."

"What set ye on the man, Rob?" asked the voice of Acton. I began now, in good truth, to catch every word, for I could place one man at least.

"'T is under the rose, John, but the fellow is trying to double spy, or so the Commander-in-Chief fears. But 't is thought, too, he belongs to Clinton. The colonel took me into his confidence, and I am to try to run him to earth. I would not tell this even to you, but that I have the colonel's consent to take your help. He goes by the name of Captain Hazeltine, and as sure as there is a God in heaven, I will come up with the man yet. It grows now to be a personal thing 'twixt him and me!"

"Then the Lord help him!" interrupted the other. And at that I was pulled by the sleeve and marched into the room.

As we passed through the door, I caught a sudden exclamation, and, turning, recognised the man I had helped on the highway, dressed now in a lieutenant's uniform, and knew he recognised me. Well, we should see what might be the outcome of it all; and if I were to have spoken my mind then, I cared not a tinker's dam.

"Number 12!" called out a deep and, to me just then, irritating voice. "Report for examination!"

I only saw in the morning sunshine that the room was filled with a number of commissioned and non-commissioned officers, and was about to move to the place allotted to me, when he who called himself Acton stepped up and frankly shook my hand.

"Ah, my friend, here you are! Rob," said he, with calm disregard of the examining officer near by, "Rob, here is the man who kept me from the worms."

"That man!" muttered the other. He had a straight figure, a fine, strong face, pale, a little sombre in expression, but to the full extent what the voice had intimated. "Nay, friend," he added dejectedly; "'t is no more like the other than you or I."

"Gentlemen," said the officer sharply, "order, an it please you. We must proceed with the examinations. Your name, sir!" turning to me.

"Merton Balfort," said I.

"No middle name?"

"No."

"I respect that man's parents," said Acton in a stage whisper. "One of us is spared a middle name."

"'T is necessary to have order here, gentlemen," cried the officer sharply.

"Quite right, too," nodded Acton, with mock seriousness.

"Your home, sir!"

"Massachusetts Colony," said I.

"What town?"

"Boston."

"The Cradle of Liberty — next to Virginia," murmured Acton in his ponderous whisper, which drew a smile from every one present.

"Lieutenant, I shall clear this room if order cannot be maintained!"

Then the nervous strain I was labouring under became too much for me.

"Sir," said I, turning to Acton, "I beg that you will let the examination proceed. You asked me to call on you, and I do so now."

"Your age?" cried the examining officer loudly.

"Twenty-two."

"Occupation?"

"Lieutenant in the division of General Israel Putnam."

"You are a soldier of the Colonies?"

"Aye, a soldier of the Colonies," I said, raising my voice; for 't was beyond me to keep calm longer under this questioning, and, as I have already said, I was come to that frame of mind where I cared not a whit what might come of it all.

Then fell a bombshell into that company.

"I do not believe it!" half muttered the officer.

That cooled me at once, and I replied:

"That is the remark of a coward, sir."

"You call me — he calls me coward, coward!" roared the examiner, jumping up and thumping his desk, while a dead silence fell over the whole company.

"'T is further the remark of a bad officer and a weak man."

"God help me, what dost say?" cried the man again.

"I say that I ask to be taken to the commander of this fort. 'T is said I must be examined. I say 'Very well, proceed; examine!' and you begin by giving me the lie, when, as man to man, I have no retaliation. You are, therefore, a weak man and a coward. You say this instead of putting to paper my examination, for your superior and better to read and judge. 'T is the method of a bad officer. You see, 't is simple enough."

"That is a brave man," came over the room in the deep tones I had heard conversing but now with Lieutenant Acton. "He speaks the truth."

"Why, you impudent scoundrel!" cried the infuriated officer. "Do you know whom you address?" He was too astonished to do more than stare at me in amazement. But I was bent on giving vent to the hours of pent-up misery I had just passed through, and it did my soul good to say so.

"In my Colony, when there comes a prisoner and shows by his manner that he has aught of importance to say, he is taken to the commanding officer. Evidently the military discipline of Verplancks is of a different sort."

"Sergeant!" roared the man. "Sergeant! Here, take this — this —" He fell over himself in his endeavour to speak. "Take this — man away, and put him under guard!"

At that, two men stepped forward, and the unknown friend of Acton said in a cold voice that seemed to command immediate attention:

"Captain, with your permission, I would speak a word concerning this man."

"And what business is it of yours?" demanded his superior. "You will retire, sir, at once!"

The slightest trace of a frown spread over the serious face, and the man turned even a little whiter, while his voice, calm as before, seemed to cut the air in the room with its decisive tone.

"This is the case of the examination of a prisoner taken at the picket line. He has the right of witness and counsel. I act as both with my friend, Lieutenant Acton."

I turned to him in wonder; but he fixed his cold eyes on the examining officer and kept them there. Every one instinctively drew up by the desk, with that silent, mysterious movement that makes no sound but means so much at times — the movement that precedes some coming event.

"Lieutenant Curtis, you will understand that you do not conduct this examination!" said the officer, trying to control himself, but with his voice rising as he proceeded. "I do, however; and, by God, sir, I'll continue to do so! Do you retire at once, or I will place you under arrest."

"Oaths have no place in an examination, sir. 'T is, therefore, in bad taste, and in contradiction to martial law —"

"Sergeant," cried the examining officer, with blazing eyes and flushed cheeks.

"I appear for this prisoner," interrupted the imperturbable man, now the only one in the room who appeared perfectly composed and calm.

"Appear for the devil in hell, if you like, but you appear for no one here!"

"And I tell you that no law in this army permits you under such conditions to tell a prisoner he is a liar."

"Sergeant, arrest Lieutenant Curtis!" yelled the stupefied officer.

"Gentlemen," said Curtis, turning to the silent but interested spectators, "is this a court, or is it perchance a collection of the benighted insane?" and a cold smile drew back the corners of his mouth. Who or what was this remarkable person? He was the picture of a calm, dignified gentleman; and yet he defied military discipline, no matter how basely applied, without the slightest apparent concern, and all on account of a man whom he saw now for the first time.

"Sergeant, arrest that man!" sounded through the room again. Every one waited, and at last the sergeant approached Lieutenant Curtis and saluted him apologetically.

There was the space of an instant, when the air was charged with portentous possibilities, and then an orderly entered and handed a note to the dazed examiner, which he, after reading with a reddening face, threw down on his desk; then, turning to the sergeant, he cried out:

"Take the prisoner to headquarters! And mark you, *Mr.* Merton Balfort, if you *should* turn out to be an officer of any — *any*, mind ye — any army of the earth, I 'll have ye out, sir, by God, I will!" And down came his fist, spilling the sand from the box by his inkstand and sounding through the room.

Something had happened, surely, for I was therewith led away out through the camp, musing on the extraordinary character of this military examination, but more especially on the remarkable man who had defied it. Here and there, as I walked along, stood farmhouses and barns and any sort of building turned into officers' quarters, or stabling room for horses, and rows of huts and tents for the infantry and cavalry of Colonel Livingstone's command.

It was, to my mind, as cleanly a camp, as good to look upon, as I had seen; but in reality there was little to grow gay over about it. Men moved here and there in ragged clothes, that bore but pitiable resemblance to uniforms, and wherever I got a glimpse into a hut or a tent, only the bare necessities of life were in view. As I walked along between two soldiers, there came to me the two men, Acton and his friend, who, whether according to the code of discipline or not I cannot tell, walked by my side.

The jovial Acton thanked me in his own way for the little service chance had enabled me to do him, and presented me to his friend, Robert Curtis. From the time I had heard the man's voice he drew me to him, and now that I saw his serious face, marked

by the lines of some sorrow or care, I took more
and more to him.

These two men spoke to me each in his own way
as we walked across the camp. And each in his
own way gave me the encouragement that two manly
beings can impart in unaffected ways. There was
little said, but I knew that here were two men such as
I had not yet met in my short life.

So we came to the country mansion that Livingstone
used as his headquarters, and I was ushered into the
library, or office, where I stood before the commander
of the Verplancks detachment of Washington's thin
line that ran from Philadelphia, by way of Morris-
town and West Point, into New England. It was
a detachment ever ready for a movement of Clinton's,
ever watching; but to a close observer, almost hope-
lessly spread out, and by three quarters less than
what it should have been in numbers.

"You have been insulting my officer, sir, I see,"
said he, after questioning me as to my station in
life.

"You are misinformed, sir," I answered.

"How so? I am reading here."

"Any of the witnesses will tell you the facts;"
and I repeated them.

He sat a moment, looking out of the window in
some thought, and then continued:

"You fired on a picket. That is severely punish-
able in martial law."

"I realise that fully, sir," I said. "But I was
hurrying in the darkness, and saw the muzzle of a

gun suddenly thrust before me. 'T was instinctive
to defend myself."

"These letters, what are they?"

"As you see, sir. One to me from General Putnam.
The other to General Washington, which you can
read as well as I."

"It is in cipher. Read it to me."

"I do not know the code."

"Then I can send it on to him."

"In that case 't will mean little, as I am instructed
to add certain details to it."

"You can tell them to me."

"With your pardon, Colonel Livingstone, I can
tell them to no one but the Commander-in-Chief.
And, sir, these reports are of such importance that
I urge you to send me on to him, under guard if
you choose, as soon as possible. 'T will work little
harm," I added, smiling, "even should I prove to
be a spy."

Again he sat for some moments pondering. Then,
rising, he rang a bell, and, bidding an orderly call
a Captain Burton, he gave that officer orders to have
me taken to General Arnold.

"General Arnold!" cried I involuntarily.

"And why not, sir?" demanded he sharply, turning suddenly upon me and fixing his clear eyes on
my face.

"Why not, indeed, except that it will cause unnecessary delay."

"That is for me to decide," he answered haughtily,
and turned away without more ado.

"Ah, friend Balfort, I am glad to see you again,"
cried Acton, as I left the house with the sergeant
some moments later. But I could say little to the
two who stood waiting for me, and within a short
time I was riding north between two other horsemen
— a sergeant and a trooper — having silently shaken
these two new friends by the hand and nodded my
farewell to them.

Arnold's headquarters I knew to be in the house
once the property of a Tory named Robinson, situ-
ated just across the Hudson from West Point. Fishkill lay beyond, I knew not how far. At this point
I got my head to thinking how I might rid myself
of this escort and ride, or walk, past the traitor's
house to the Commander-in-Chief.

It was now come to four in the afternoon of the
22nd. The attack was for the 28th. Here lay six
days. It must be done. Aye, and done quickly!
And then my thoughts turned to the two escorting me.
Neither had any brilliancy sitting upon his brow.
The sergeant, upon my right, carried the two papers.
Even now I could see them, with Livingstone's despatches, bulging from his pocket. The men had
pistols in saddle-holsters, and I had none.

Then of a sudden came to me an idea, and I have
to this day never discovered how it turned out so
well; for, to tell honest fact, 't was as wild a scheme
as ever entered my poor head.

It was just after this that my two companions
began to discover that their prisoner was, of a surety,
no horseman. He often grasped the saddle roughly;

when the beast trotted a bit, the bumping of the cap-
tive was disgraceful; in point of fact, it appeared that
this prisoner could not have ridden a horse six times
in his life.

It tickled the soul of the cavalry sergeant beyond
measure. The tedious ride contained possibilities of
amusement.

"Ye ain't got none too much of the horseman in
yer bones, have ye?" laughed he presently. "There
ye go agin — ho! ho!" as the prisoner's horse shied
and bumped his own good steed. "Ye must hold
firmer by the knees. So! Sit so! straighter!" and
he leaned over and put his hand on the other's
shoulder.

I will not deny that a certain gleam appeared in
the prisoner's eye.

"I see! 'T is simple, too," said the latter. But
the beast sidled up to the third horseman of the
party and pushed him to the side of the road.

"Have a care, here, my sportsman!" cried he,
laughing good-humouredly.

Now, by chance, the road became hilly, and curved
through the trees and open fields; when, without
warning, the foolish prisoner let go of the reins and
grabbed his saddle with both hands, and the disgusted animal under him went here and there, amidst
the laughter of the sergeant, who broke into a brisk
trot, thus adding to the amusement of himself and
his friend. He drew a few yards ahead of the other
two. Another turn of the road was in sight, when
the prisoner's horse gave a prodigious leap towards

the trooper near by, and there was a grab at his saddle pistols. A report sang out before either he or his sergeant could stop laughing. The trooper's horse turned a somersault and rolled over in the mud with its rider.

As the sergeant turned in his saddle, I had him covered with the other pistol. He saw the muzzle of the gun not four feet behind him.

"Ride on, man! Put in the spur! Lively — lively! Or you'll ride to kingdom come!"

'T would be untrue to say that the humorous sergeant was not in an embarrassing position. If he turned, he caught the glint of the gun. If he rode on, he must have felt it pointed at the small of his back. He had not only humour; he had wisdom. He obeyed in silence and rode on.

After the pace had been maintained three or four minutes, I bade him pull up and came along by his side.

"Hold your hands above your head! Now dismount — aha! Keep thy hands up, man! Jump down!"

This he did, his eye never leaving the opening of the barrel.

"Give me those letters and your pistol and sword."

"How can I, then, without moving my hands?"

"Move one."

This was done.

"Now, sergeant, take off your clothes."

For an instant the poor fellow showed fight, but 't was useless, and, with a choking groan, he took off his uniform, and we changed clothes then and there by the country roadside.

A few moments later Sergeant Balfort, your humble servant, who shows his cheap conceit in telling this tale of his own great prowess, was riding hard northward towards Arnold's house — which was on the way to Fishkill, be it understood — and a countryman in a suit of clothes I was sorry to lose was standing in the road scratching his head, while a good horse was running well down the road towards Verplancks.

CHAPTER VII

GEORGE WASHINGTON

IT was an hour later that the horse which had brought me from Verplancks carried me by the Robinson house, filled now with so much more villainy than could ever have been there through a Tory's principles. Robinson, at least, had stuck by his opinions and acknowledged them, bad as they were. But here was one who was professing patriotism and living a lie, and who, if I did not hasten, would endanger the existence of the whole country.

It was a further spur to speed, and I rode on the faster, urging the animal again to his best. By seven o'clock at night, with never a stop for rest or food, we came up with the village of Fishkill. There was no difficulty in finding headquarters; but there another disappointment awaited me. General Washington had left a few days before for Hartford. This was told me only after I had satisfied an aide in charge of headquarters that I had pressing business with the general.

"How far may it be to Hartford?" I asked.

"Good Lord, man, it's a hundred miles!"

"It matters not. I must get there as soon as possible," I said. "Could you let me have a good horse?"

He looked at me for an instant. Then I opened the letter from Putnam and bade him read. It was quite enough. I had the horse in a few moments, and was away again. The general had gone by the lower road, which I learned branched off the Hudson River road just to the south of the village, and the clock on the meeting house in Fishkill struck nine as I finally made the turn eastward.

The beast I had was indeed a good one, and he carried me steadily and well. It was futile to hurry him beyond his endurance, for the good animal must keep me moving for two days. I was cooling down gradually and gaining my ordinary powers of reasoning things out, and there were hours in which to reflect. At half past two we pulled up at the Tottern Arms inn for a few moments' rest, for the good horse had not dropped into a trot in three hours and a half.

It would seem as if the devil had his hand in this business; for I could wake no one. But by dint of much thumping and kicking on the door of the inn, and a vigorous howling out for some one, I got at last a nightcap out of the window, and no very civil reply to my demands. Still, in fifteen minutes or more, the door opened, and I asked for any food they had while I put my questions.

"How far to Hartford?" cried the tavern-keeper. "Bless my soul, I don't know! Jennie, how far would it be now to Hartford? What was that we heard of Hartford last week?"

"Why, them big officers talked of it," answered a woman in a short wrapper, her nightshift showing beneath it.

"Who?" cried I. The dim old room, lit now by a single candle, prevented my seeing clearly, and I approached the woman so suddenly, so intent on what I had caught, that she fled up the steep stairway, and could not be persuaded to come down again.

After much pleading, however. I learned that several officers — one of enormous stature and great eyes, with a wide mouth and white periwig — had stopped there last Friday, six days before, on their way to Hartford, evidently, from what they had said.

"Good people," cried I, standing at the foot of the stairs and addressing the woman above and the man by the table, "good people, that was General Washington and his staff, and I must catch them within two days!"

"No! Ye don't say so!" came from the head of the stairs. "What said I to ye, Henry? Did I not tell ye, man, 't was a great company, and you with your dirty apron on at the time! Lord love ye, Henry, ye will never move up in life with ye —"

"My dear, good woman," cried I again, "said they aught else? Think! Canst remember anything of their return?"

"Not much," grunted the old lady. "To think that Henry should have talked with the great man in his apron and his old breeks!"

"What said they, madam? Tell me, and Henry shall have a new apron; aye, and another pair of breeks!"

"Of good corduroy?"

"Yes, yes! And two pairs."

"Why little enough said they; but it seems to me that I did hear the big man speak as how they 'd come home by the upper road."

"Here — here, man! Here's that will buy thee breeks with four legs, and now, in God's name, which way lies the upper road?"

The horse was half done up, but 't was little more than another quarter of an hour when I had, by their direction, got him into a small country lane — rutted as only such lanes in this country of ours can be — that ran northward, and should bring me to the upper road.

And a heartless ride it was to join that highway. I love a horse, more especially a good one, and always have. And the pace I put that good animal to had its effect on me. I talked to him. I let him drink at every stream we forded. But go he must, and did, at the long reaching gallop. And then, with a surprising suddenness, we came out on the unmistakable highway. Off to the eastward struck the clang of a church bell — one — two — three — four. I turned that way, and stopped under a creaking sign in the midst of a village. Good news this time! No doubt of them; they had passed here the night before. Hour after hour we pushed on, till at last we reached the great road running up and down the Hudson. It was then after five o'clock, and daylight had begun to warm the morning air. Still there lay ten miles to Fishkill.

It was done in less than an hour. The horse grew into my heart with his steady nerve. No sign at head-

quarters! The commander had been there, tired and
ready to rest, when he had been called south to the
headquarters of the West Point commander. And
so on I went towards the Robinson house.

It was close upon nine o'clock as I made the old
house close under the side of Sugar Loaf, and turned
up into the drive that led to the side door. It was
patent to the eye that something unusual was going
on. Horses stood about, held by orderlies. On the
piazza walked several officers, aides, as I guessed,
talking together, and voices could be heard from
within. Just as I pulled up, came the pitiable shriek
of a woman.

No one paid the slightest attention to me; and,
dismounting, I started to run to the door, when the
good horse, who had carried me so far, quietly lay
down without a groan. I could not pause, for I felt
that if I stood still long the nerve would be lacking
to set me moving again. It does not behoove a man
to magnify his own doings by telling of his troubles,
but 't is no weakness in me to say that I walked into
that house, pushing aside several men who would have
stopped me, in a kind of dream. Each in turn looked
at me, and then, as I pushed him aside without a word,
I caught an exclamation, but met no further resist-
ance from him.

So on into a great, long, low dining-room. One
look told me my chief was found; the huge, sombre
man, the great face with its sad eyes, the wide, straight
mouth — there he stood by the window. At the moment of my entrance he turned and said to a military

companion in a calm, self-possessed voice, that was still full of grief and sorrow:

"General, whom can we trust now?"

Then the three occupants of the room turned and saw me.

"What do you here, sir?" asked the stern voice of him just called "General."

"I must speak with the Commander-in-Chief at once, sir," I answered.

"You cannot now. Retire at once!"

"One moment, Knox," said a deep voice. Then, turning to me, Washington added, "Here he is, my man. What is it?"

"Your Excellency," said I, looking at the others, "I have something of the greatest importance to say to you."

"Well, say it quickly. These gentlemen may hear anything I can."

At this moment all heard again that woman's shriek. The general's face was immediately overcast with a look of pain.

"You said that some one was with Mrs. Arnold, Knox, did you not?" he asked.

"Yes, General. The maids are with her, and a man has gone across for a physician."

"Now, young man, speak up," said Washington again.

"I overheard, night before last, a conversation, your Excellency, between—a British officer—Major André—"

"Who is captured and in custody," interrupted Washington.

"And — and — " I hesitated.

"Well?"

"And Major-General Benedict Arnold — "

"Who has this morning escaped to the British lines."

"Escaped?"

"Escaped."

"It is fate!"

"Sergeant," said the general solemnly, "'t is the will of God." This was spoken in a voice filled with infinite grief, sorrow, and disappointment. "But the young soldier is ill," he added hastily, for 't was like the last blow of a week's hardship, and I grasped the breakfast table to steady myself. "Tell me what you heard."

"I overheard a conversation between these two officers," I managed to say, "below Haverstraw, night before last. I crossed the river and tried to reach you at Fishkill. I was captured at Teller's Point, and treated as a spy, because letters were found on me. I escaped from the guard, took a horse, and have been riding since yesterday afternoon to catch you. You were not at Fishkill — I took the lower road for Hartford, and missed you; I found my mistake, went across to the upper road, missed you again, and — rode back! I have covered a hundred miles since five yesterday, and now — now I am too late! It is fate! It could not have been otherwise!"

Several exclamations had burst from the third occupant of the room as I spoke, and he muttered to himself at the end:

"*Mordieu*, but that was a brave ride!"

"It must have been, indeed, Lafayette," said Washington. Then, turning to me, he said:

"You are hungry and worn out, Sergeant. Sit down and eat."

"I have not eaten in twenty-six hours," I answered, "but I cannot wait. I must, I *will* find that man and bring him back."

A sudden gleam shot into the general's eye. "Patience, young man, patience!" he said in a voice that would make a man ashamed of his own weakness. "We will find him. And he will be punished, never fear, whether we find him or not, and you shall have your chance! But who are you?" And he looked at me with a glance that seemed to take in all my thoughts.

"I am called Merton Balfort."

"You are an American soldier, too?"

"Yes, your Excellency. I am a lieutenant, serving under General Putnam."

"You have come from him recently?" asked Washington suddenly.

"Yes, your Excellency, I am here to deliver these two letters to you from him;" and I handed him the two notes.

"You may sit down, Lieutenant," said the general, as he took the letters and moved towards the window. But, whatever the desire might be, I would not sit in the presence of this man.

As he read the note from General Putnam to myself, the chief glanced once or twice at me with a thoughtful look, and then went on reading. Opening the other note, and discovering it to be in cipher, he took a small book from his pocket and, with General Knox's assistance, made out its meaning. As they slowly discovered its import, the two generals conversed.

"Strange," said the commander; "and Rochambeau knew nothing of this before yesterday."

"The letter is dated only a few days ago, and it speaks of the affair as taking place off Boston."

"True, he cannot have been informed. Lieutenant," asked Washington, "do you know what this note speaks of?"

"Not absolutely, your Excellency. Only in a general way."

"What is it?"

"That General Putnam has advices from Boston, saying that British war ships are appearing singly off the coast here and there."

"That is correct."

"That they seem to be combining into a fleet."

"Also correct, but a mark signifies here that you will add something."

"The general wished me to say, your Excellency, that he felt sure that there was a plan to retake Newport, or to make some attack on Boston."

"The note also says he advises having the fleet watched."

"He thinks that an outpost should be established beyond Cape Cod, both at the north and towards the south."

"That sounds reasonable and could be done," said General Knox thoughtfully.

"Evidently," said the Commander-in-Chief to Lafayette, "it is a fleet sent out by George the Third to cope with Rochambeau."

"I do not understand M. Rochambeau not having heard," answered the latter.

"He could not know, your Excellency," I interrupted, "since the news was brought in by one of the Boston fishermen, who had been chartered to watch out beyond Cape Cod."

"Could such a watch be kept up along the coast?" asked Washington.

"There is no doubt of it, your Excellency," said I.

"Lieutenant," said Washington, after a moment's thought, "you will return to Colonel Livingstone, and hold yourself in readiness to set out."

I saluted, but hesitated, with a longing to get in a word.

"You wish to say something?"

"I am an escaped prisoner of the colonel's, and he holds me as a spy. I was being sent on as such to General Arnold when I escaped."

"To Arnold?" cried Lafayette with enthusiasm. "Ah, that is sublime! Sent to Arnold! He escapes —he rides a hundred miles, and neither eats nor drinks! Ah, that is glorious, young man!" And the Frenchman, whom I now knew for General Lafayette, patted me gently on the shoulder. "Glorious! glorious! We should have such men in France to-day!"

"Nay, General," said Washington sadly; "we need

them too much here." Then he wrote a few words
on a bit of paper and handed it to me.

"That will save you from any rough handling."

I stood for a moment looking into the commander's
careworn but kindly face.

"What! There is still something on your mind?"

"Yes, your Excellency."

"Speak out, man! You have spoken to such good
purpose that I can well afford to hear more."

"General Washington," I cried, "I demand permission to recapture that traitor to the American
cause."

There was a moment of silence. The three generals looked at one another, and that same fierce gleam
came into the commander's eyes for another instant.

"Lieutenant Balfort," said Washington slowly and
solemnly, with that same sagacious but kindly look,
"take what food and rest you need. Then return to
Colonel Livingstone's command, and hold yourself
in readiness night and day to set out on whatever
mission the success of our cause or my will may
command."

I saluted and turned away; for I had learned enough
of this man by hearsay to know that he neither liked
nor brooked discussion.

"And now, gentlemen," he added in that even tone
that never seemed to leave him, "now, gentlemen,
since Mrs. Arnold is ill, and the general is not here
to entertain us, let us sit down and breakfast without
ceremony."

I went into the open air, and, as if to add the last

straw to my strained nerve, came upon the good horse that had so steadily, so bravely, carried me mile after mile. His cold body, bridled and saddled, lying there on the grass, completely unnerved me; and I sat me down on the porch before all those standing there, and put my head in my arms. A man can stand but so much, after all.

6

CHAPTER VIII

IN WHICH I AM BIDDEN TO ENTER A FORBIDDEN
HOUSE

"SO you 're stationed with us now, my friend?"
asked Acton a couple of days later, as we sat
in Lieutenant Curtis's quarters in the upper
story of Colonel Livingstone's house.

I told him that he was right. For, on presenting the
Commander-in-Chief's note to the colonel, the latter
had shaken me cordially by the hand, and told me that
no one could be more pleased than he over the result.
It turned out that when he read Putnam's note, while
I was undergoing my first examination in the guard-
house, he felt that something was wrong; and, realising that Washington often had agents at work whom
no one else knew, he had called me to him, judged for
himself, and done what he could to help me along. It
goes without saying that Arnold's treason was as unknown to him as to every one else; and, as I learned
now, if I had told him the whole story, he would not
have thought of believing it.

Then I had been placed on his staff as an aide, to
do what might come within my power, while I awaited
further orders from General Washington. And I had
looked up the only two men I had made friends with
during my short sojourn at the fort. They appeared

— each in his own way — glad to have me with them again, the one boisterous and full of regard for a man who, however unconsciously, had been the means of saving him from possible death, the other calm, cool, serious, and reserved, a gentleman to his finger tips. Curtis, indeed, haunted me a little by a strange twist which his face had now and again of looking familiar, as if I had known him long ago in a past age, when he wore other garments. Nay, 't was more than the face. The voice, the little mannerisms that a man will always carry about him, would all now and then bring this peculiar prior existence to my mind.

Yet it was all intangible and curious — so strangely so that I almost of necessity tried to learn something of his life and antecedents. Here again I was baffled. No one — not a soul in that regiment — knew aught of him back of a couple of years, when he had joined with a lieutenant's commission and been placed under Captain Jacob Barnes, who commanded a company of Livingstone's foot. Distinguished service had raised him to the colonel's staff.

Acton, whom I immediately came to look on as a friend — a friend who has remained the same through thirty-odd years — told me what little I could learn of Robert Curtis. He himself was the son of an old Jamestown Colony family, and had drifted into Livingstone's regiment through a Captain Henry, whose lieutenant he now was. And it appeared that Curtis had little to do with any one but this one Southern officer. According to John, Curtis had no lack of money, but spent little or nothing. The frank fellow, after their acquaintance became established, had asked his friend concerning his own family, and had been cut short by Curtis's gloomy face and his answer that he had none.

Neither could he learn where the young man came from, nor why he was weighed down so by such sorrow as prevented him from taking part in any of the recreations of camp life. He never laughed; sometimes he would smile. He never talked to any great extent; but on occasion, when some military or political subject came up, he could talk freely and well, with the knowledge of a travelled and a studied man. He lived, in fact, a life apart from the life of the camp, a camp where I soon found that, in spite of the lack of money, there was no lack of amusement of every kind. Yet, withal, Curtis was never brusk; no one was too low for his courtesy; no officer could browbeat him with the rights of discipline when the higher rights were on his side. He had fought Captain Barnes and wounded him, because the latter had ruined a country wench near by, and then tried to browbeat Curtis when the latter criticised him to his face. Several times he had, I learned, called a superior to account, as on the day of my arrest.

John Acton, or Jack, as I, like all the world, at once called him, was of another type. Huge in size, he was big in every way — open-hearted, open-handed, full of a great, hearty laugh, careless of himself and all else, fond of a jovial evening, but as big in his sense of honesty and chivalry as he was in stature.

They made a strange pair, these two. Yet, perhaps
by their very opposites, they were drawn together. My
dropping in with them was all Acton's doing. Curtis
I should never have known otherwise; for he did his
best to avoid meeting any one excepting Acton. 'Twas
the latter who took me to his heart at once, and so
I saw Curtis and became so strangely fascinated by
the peculiarly familiar look and manner he seemed to
have that, perforce, he had to tolerate me; and in a
few days I came to the habit of being with these two
men whenever we were off duty.

In such a camp, lifelong friendships and enmities
are quickly made, and the existence of our American
officers of those days, filled always with work, was relieved by the social life of little cliques and groups.
Such an one was I now taken into, and before long
we three had agreed, among ourselves, that whenever
occasion arose for special duty on the part of any one
of us, that one would if possible secure the other two
to help him carry through the affair.

The especially important case in point was the capture of a certain man called Captain Hazeltine. I had
overheard something of him that morning in the guard-
house, and learned now that the man had become a
sort of mania with Curtis. The latter had distinguished himself on several occasions in carrying out
special work, and a direct order had now come from
the Commander-in-Chief for Lieutenant Curtis to
watch and, if possible, take this man. I learned, too,
that he was thought to be a spy of Clinton's—a Tory
working with the English, in other words; but that

he had passed for a short time as a private agent of Washington, coming well recommended from two friends in New York. The Commander-in-Chief, however, with his unerring sagacity, had finally come to suspect the man, and had then lost him of a sudden.

Curtis had seen him now four times, but never face to face, only in the darkness. And the way the man had eluded him had hurt the young lieutenant's pride, besides giving his strong, serious nature a difficult task that fitted into his desire for hard labour of any sort.

"I'll come up with the man, if it takes the powers of hell to do it," he declared one night, after we had spent the evening covering a bit of the country to the eastward of Teller's Point.

"Egad, Rob, I pity him," cried Acton, "for ye'll come up with him some day, and then will there be a short but unpleasant hour for him."

"If ever I meet him," said the other calmly, "'t will be a short affair, for 't is between him and me now; and, if you'll believe it, I'm blessed if I do not think he knows it."

"Ye'll do it, by Gad, Rob, ye'll do it, sure!" said the other with that boundless confidence of an open, enthusiastic nature in one who is always reserved and unenthusiastic to a fault.

So in the ten days that followed my arrival we spent half the time scouring the country, looking for this ghost with the cape coat and the phantom horse. To confess truth, I had some doubts of the importance of the work, which showed how little I knew of the in-

triguing and under-current work going on at this
otherwise strangely stagnant period of the war. 'Twas
on such an expedition that Acton had nearly lost his
life when I chanced along; and, in fact, 'twas no
child's play to roam about the country to the south
of us, infested as it was with all the outlaws of the
northern part of the Colonies.

These villains preyed on any one, and we were good
meat for them. Two or three running fights we had
in these ten days, as it was, but without results of any
kind, save the lesson of knowing when to run away.
Yet could Acton never get this better part of valour
into his head; for 'twas always a hard task to make
him retire. As on the day I first met him, he would
brighten up at the prospect of a fight, and would tackle
any number of Skinners that might fall in with us
with a laugh on his lips and joy in his heart. And
then, when we had finally got him away, once actually
leading his horse against his will, he would curse us
roundly for an hour, and then beg our pardon!

Yet with all this the time dragged with me, for I
had hoped to get a commission to search for Arnold,
and each day that passed made this more hopeless.
Once we heard that he lay in New York; again, that
he had gone to England; still again, that he had joined
Cornwallis in the South. I had, of course, told my
story to my two friends, and we had here again agreed
to work together, should I ever gain permission to go
forth in search of him. The idea brought more life and
colour to Curtis's face than anything I had witnessed
since making his acquaintance; for, cool though he

was and little given to enthusiasm, this was a work
after his own heart. In fact, his mind seemed gradually to settle upon that, too, as a piece of work he must
have a hand in.

Then, too, my mind would continually hark back to
a face that would not down from my thoughts, and I
wondered night after night as I lay in my bed — for
the colonel's aides actually did have beds — what she
did now, and now; where she was; what might be
her sorrow and trouble that had taken her from her
home, and why fate should have set the insurmount-
able barrier of a great war between us. Of the episode
of Gowan's Tavern in which one James Marvin had
taken so significant a part, I thought but little and
spoke not at all, because, indeed, it meant naught.
And yet 't was a strange satisfaction that would run
through my blood, to think that this one unknown
woman of all others in the world had stood beside me
there, had ridden with me the next morning, and,
whatever she might have felt, had certainly trusted me.
If I could see her once again, under happy circum-
stances! If I could watch the sudden changes of mood
fly one after another across her fair face! Aye, if I
could! If I could! If —

And in walked Curtis with his usual careless step
and undisturbed countenance, to say:

"Get your kit together, lad. We go on something
worth while this night."

Without a word, I took my sword from the corner
and got pistol and boots ready. 'T was only a moment,
and we went over to his room, where sat Jack Acton,
ready as well.

"*We passed out of camp into the night*"

"We take twenty men, and ride south. Are you ready?"

"Why twenty men, Rob?" asked Acton. "Let us do it alone, whatever it may be."

"We shall need them all. Nothing more here. The walls can hear and talk of it."

"Still, I do not see," went on the big fellow; but he followed after.

Outside, over by the barracks, with his usual precision, Curtis pointed out to us the troop of twenty men, ready mounted, and our horses standing by. I was up on Roger at once, for I had the dear old nag again safe and sound. And we rode away south, giving the word and a greeting to the pickets as we passed out of camp into the night and the uncertain neutral country. The command had been passed along for silence, and so we rode hour by hour steadily southward, until by the distance my heart began to beat faster, for by now I had begun to know the country, and I saw we must be fast nearing a certain fated house. If I could but see her once!

"This way, Jack and Balfort," said Curtis out of the darkness; and we moved a hundred yards in advance of the troop. "We are getting near the place."

"And I should like to know —" began Acton.

"Why we are here? Well, listen. There is an impression that an attempt has been planned to recapture André, who was to have been taken to-night down this side of the river and carried over to the other bank, on his way to Tappan for trial. The colonel had word from headquarters this evening, at six, that the plans are changed.

"André goes from West Point without crossing, and we are to take the British squad, or troop, that will come here to take him. They may be on hand now. They may not come till later, as the prisoner was to cross about four in the morning. At all events, the meeting, or place of concealment, will be in a house here at Gowan's Ferry, which I will show you." My heart gave a double jump as he went on: "We shall divide into three parties, one going south, one eastward, and the other making an attempt to enter the house."

"Give me the house, Curtis," said I quickly; "I want work badly."

He said nothing, and we moved on; when, as if by magic, I recognised in the darkness the wood-lined road, and in another moment, coming out into the open, I knew the house where I had last seen Deborah Philipse. Turning to Curtis to urge my point now with added fervour, I caught a fierce yet mournful look in his face as he gazed with wide eyes at the old mansion, and the request froze on my lips. He looked long as we waited for the troop to come up, and then, as if by an effort, turned his face towards me and said:

"Balfort, take six men and enter that house, if you can. Once there, conceal your men and take anything and anybody who tries to enter. I go south to meet them with six troopers, and Acton will cover the country to the eastward with the others."

I said not a word, but, as I picked the sergeant and five men, I fervently and silently thanked heaven.

CHAPTER IX

THE REAL MOUSE IN THE TRAP

I COULD not help wondering, after my two friends disappeared in the darkness, at the peculiar chance of fate, or whatever one might wish to call it, that left me now standing here by the house I had so longed to enter but a few short days ago, with orders now to enter it, but the inclination to do so gone. Gone, did I say? Nay, hardly that, for if any one of us entered there, it must be I; and, whatever might be the real reason of her going there, I could not let her be taken in arrest as a common spy.

Why she should be there now, I did not want to guess. And, indeed, the doubt of it growing on me, I turned to the sergeant of the troop and looked him over: a grizzly bearded old campaigner, used to wars, but honest and a stalwart Colonial, I 'd be bound. 'T was, in fact, the picket who had taken me the night I reached Teller's Point. What would he do with Mistress Philipse, if he found her there? I did not like to think, but spoke to him instead:

"Callahan," said I, "know ye why we 're here?"

"That I do not, liftinint," said he. "I am ordered here, and here I be. Indade, sir, I 've outgrown askin' quistions."

"You can keep your mouth shut well?"

"Ask the liftinint," and he jerked his thumb over his shoulder towards the departing troop.

"Good! Remember that, should the time come! — take now two men and go around that house to the left. Leave two more here concealed near the road, and let the other go with me to the right."

"Aye, sir."

"We must enter that house, search it, get what may be inside, and lie low for more. And look sharp, for 't is like there be no less than a dozen red-coats there now, watching for us."

"Aye, sir," said he, saluting again.

"If you hear or see aught, leave a man and make a wide circuit till you meet me."

So we started away, crawling on our stomachs and keeping a bright eye on the gloomy house that appeared to be dark from top to bottom, and that contained God knew what.

Fortunately for us, there had grown up a wealth of underbrush on all sides, and by keeping well within this I turned the first corner, skirted the broad side of the square mansion, and, nothing appearing amiss, moved slowly and laboriously on, turning the second corner.

There at last was a light shining from an open window in what appeared to be a room adjoining the kitchen, in an ell, or extension, of the house itself. Soon I was up to it, and, seeing it unoccupied, made bold to enter, sending one man to call the others with Callahan.

Silence reigned throughout the house and nothing changed in the few moments that passed till, silently, one by one, the five men and Callahan slid over the sill and stood waiting my instructions.

"Some one is here, or this is a trap," said I, in a whisper. "We must act quickly, or be caught ourselves."

"'T is simple enough, sir," said the old man, coolly.

"And how?"

"Lay another thrap. An ye'll give me lave —"

"Go on," said I quickly.

"You, Durgin," ordered Callahan of one of his men, "git out o' that winder into the grass, and give us warnin' wid a tap on the glass ef annything turns up. You, Ballard, shut the winder and draw thim curtins, and do yez stand by to git the signal. You two take thim two doors and douse annywan, the divil cares who, that shows his red nose through. Douse him wid yer coats over the head and when ye git him, stick yer knee in the pit of his stomach," all this in a whisper, with a quick look here and there, and gestures that alone told what he wanted. "An' now, yer honour, we'll take this door that goes God knows where — st! Phwat the divil's that?"

'T was a step coming along the hall, a light, stealthy, though quick step. In a moment Callahan and I were behind the door, and my cape was ready in his hands, held at the height of a man's head. Each of the others had taken his position silently as soon as he got his orders.

There was a moment of suspense as the steps came

towards the door. Then the door itself swung open and in an instant Callahan was on the ground on top of some one, with the cape wound around the new arrival's head.

"The Saints deliver me!" muttered the old man. "Divil take me, but it's a woman!"

And, sure, 't was so. For the door being again quietly closed, we carried her to the light, and found a woman, speechless with terror, gazing with a fascinated glare down the barrel of Callahan's pistol.

"Do not utter a sound, or you will be dead!" said I, sternly. But she did not appear to take note of anything but the pistol.

"Who's in this house?" I asked.

No answer or move on her part.

I knocked up the sergeant's pistol, much to his disgust, and touched her.

"Who is in this house?"

She looked at me in a stupid, clownish way, and then of a sudden out came a lot of gibberish that meant naught to either of us.

"Phwat's that she says?" asked Callahan. "She'll wake the dead!" And he doused her again with the cape, until she lay quiet. Then we repeated the action with the pistol and she sat silent as before. But I had caught enough to know that she spoke French.

Here we were, stumped! Not one of us knew a word of the lingo, and I could do naught but put my finger on my mouth and vigorously shake my head. French — a French maid — Mistress Philipse's maid, no doubt. Was she a bait? We should soon see.

But I must speak with her mistress first, and alone. All this passed in a moment through my mind. I bade Callahan keep the woman close, saying that I was going to explore the house, and he was to give me warning of any new arrival, or danger, by a low whistle.

So I left the dimly lighted room and found myself in a cross hall that led again into the main hall of the house. Keeping close to the wall, I worked slowly and as silently as possible around the hall, finding four great dark and silent rooms, in which the ghostly furniture stood piled in the centre. No sign nor sound of living being appeared. Then, coming to the great stairway, I drew my sword and, holding a pistol in the left hand, mounted cautiously to the second story.

Here again were more rooms, open, but vacant. Under the sill of a door leading into the wing was what seemed to be a faint light. The door opened, but in doing so it creaked with a sound that seemed to echo all over the house. Directly opposite, across another small hall, was a door, half opened, leading into a lighted room, and on the instant a voice said something in French.

'T is ever the fact that what is expected is like to be the greatest surprise, and to recognise that voice now, knowing it must come some time, gave me a sickening of the heart that kept me silent.

" Well, Adèle ? " said the voice again, louder than before.

" 'T is not Adèle, Mistress Philipse, but I, Merton Balfort. May I enter ? "

There came a sudden exclamation and a step, and the door stood wide open. There she stood in a long wrapper, with her hair down about her shoulders, — taller by inches, I remember noticing even then.

"What do you here, sir?" said she, gazing at me.

For answer I stepped into the room, took the door-handle from her, closed the door with as little noise as possible, and looked at her.

"Who are you, and what mean you by coming thus into my house?" she asked haughtily, standing away from me and drawing her gown together at the neck. Aye, the girl was beautiful under all conditions, for here she was gazing at me like a queen whose hallowed privacy had been soiled with sacrilege.

"You know me well, Mistress Philipse," said I, "and need have no fears of me."

"I know nothing of you, sir, nor do I fear you. But I bid you leave this room and this house at once, unless you are a highwayman come to rob a defenceless woman."

"You know well that is not the case. Will you be seated?"

"No! I will not!"

"I have something to say to you —"

"And I will no longer remain in your presence," and she made as if to leave the room. But I stepped before her, my own temper beginning to rise at this denial of an acquaintance which, one would think, she at least might recall.

"Mistress Philipse, I am sorry to be under the necessity of asking you to remain. I am obliged to ask you —"

"You need not ask, sir. For I will not answer a single question."

"Sit down, mistress," said I sternly. It is to this day a marvel to me how this chit of a girl could rouse my anger by her very calmness. She did not move, but said with fine scorn:

"You are then a highwayman, I see," and, following her glance, I flushed to find myself standing before her with a drawn sword in one hand and a pistol in the other. One was sheathed and the other put up in a moment, but I was upset and said nothing for a space.

"Who is in this house besides yourself and your maid?"

"An infamous scoundrel! Perchance — aye, no doubt — a highwayman! a man who has neither sense of decency, nor honour, who —"

"Who beside him? Tell me!" I cried.

"I will not speak with you further. You do not dare to remain in my presence longer!" said she, her voice rising in anger and wounded pride, and beginning to quiver with nervousness.

"Madam, you will some day regret your words," said I, hastily. "I am here to protect you " — an involuntary exclamation escaped her — "to protect you from being arrested as a spy. This house is full of British soldiers, who are" —

"Ah!" cried she, at that; "let them come to me now, then," and she rushed by me and grasped the door to open it. But I caught her as she cried out, and put my hand over her mouth and lifted her from the ground, setting her down in a large chair by the

7

table. The result was enough to distract any man. For she burst into tears, and, looking up and stamping her foot in helpless rage, she cried:

" Are you not ashamed to maltreat a woman, who is helpless! Are you not ashamed! Oh, had I a strong arm to strike you down now, making war on a weak woman!"

I was on my knees at her feet in a moment, and took her hand in mine in my excitement.

" Dear child," cried I, " God forgive me! Some day you will understand and forgive me too. I cannot do aught else. If you will but give me your word! Believe me, believe me, I would not touch a hair of your head, but tell me truthfully is this house occupied by British soldiers? Nay, do not move away! I — I must trust you. Listen! There is an attempt to take André — this house is the rendezvous — tell me you know naught of it! Oh, 't is useless to try to escape. I have the house surrounded with my men; but tell me you know naught of it, that I may protect you from my own people! Do you not see? You will be arrested as a spy!" She was sobbing, convulsively, and I could not stop her. I knew not what to do, and in the bewilderment I found myself kissing the hand that lay in mine, and begging her to stop.

Still she sobbed on. I was near at my wits' ends.

" Stop! stop! mistress; for the love of Heaven, listen to me! Well, so be it!" — for she was almost hysterical in her weeping; — " so be it," said I, rising and moving away. " There is the door. Go out and down into the very arms of my men and be taken to West Point as a spy in the employ of the British."

She was on her feet, running wildly to the door, that now stood open; and I waited to hear the result, when she stopped, as if turned to stone, for a long, low whistle came to our ears from below. I jumped to her side and grasped her arm.

"Tell me, girl, do you know aught of British in this house?"

"No," said she, looking at me in wonder.

"Then listen!"

Again came the low whistle from the hall below. I gave the signal back.

"That signal says that some one is approaching this house. Now, if you do not believe in me and do what I tell you, we shall none of us have long to live. I served you truly once. Trust me again!" and I ran to the light and blew it out. In the sudden darkness I found her and grasped her hand. She let it lie in mine, while both listened for the next sound that might come. Gradually the slight moonlight gave us some light in the room, and I turned towards her.

"Will you give me your word not to give any sign or make any noise?"

She did not reply.

"I must go downstairs; will you give it?"

Still no sign.

"Then I must trust to your sense of justice and honour."

I could not see her face, but I knew I was needed below; and so, letting her hand fall, I moved quickly

to the door. Some slight sound made me turn as I
reached it, and I was in the nick of time to see her
stealing swiftly towards the window. With a bound
I reached her, just as she raised the sash, and before
I could stop her she had cried out. Then the pity of
it all came over me, for the frail little creature began
to struggle.

"Mistress Philipse, I am here to do my duty! There
be twenty-five men and three officers within call. You
cannot possibly help the British! They are doomed
now! But I cannot — God forgive me, I will not
struggle with you! There is but one other alterna-
tive. Here is a pistol; you can easily see me. Shoot
quick and straight; for I will not go down, or take
you down to those men!" She took the revolver.
"If you fire it without hitting me, I shall use this one
on myself!"

Slowly she raised the pistol — I could see as plain
as day, now — slowly she pointed it, first at my body,
then at my throat, then my head. And it came into
my mind that my hour was, indeed, come; but there
was no trouble in my mind; for if I must go, I would
go by her hand, and that was as it should be. I
looked her steadily in the eye for a time, and then
the shining thing dropped with a clatter to the floor,
and she stood still looking into my face.

How long we stood thus, I could not tell; but we
both started as a voice came from outside the door,
whispering to me:

"Are ye there, liftinint?"

"Yes. What is it, Callahan?"

"There's twilve min a-comin' over the hill at the back of the house."

"Go down again and work your trap on them. Let in half, and cover the others. Let them have it, if anything sudden occurs."

"Yes, sir. Have ye found annywan?"

"Not a man! But I have not yet covered the whole house. There's some one in the back of the house here. Go down! I'll be with you in an instant."

I heard him mutter something about coming down now, but he went away, and we could hear his step creak on the stair.

"Do you understand now?" I asked in a whisper.

She nodded her head.

"Will you trust to me?"

Again she nodded.

"Will you — will you try to forgive me?"

"I cannot! I cannot!" she murmured, and sank back into the chair. "You have no right to treat a woman so. They are my people, too, trying to rescue a brave man — a man I know!"

"They can do nothing for him. He will not come this way, and is even now safe on the other side of the river. 'T is absolutely hopeless, mistress!" Though, in good truth, it was not so hopeless as it might seem.

So she stood a moment; and then I left her, and stole softly towards the door.

"Do not go down," came to me in hurried tones, as she moved after me. "I — I do not want — I do not dare to stay here alone!"

"But I must go down to take command of the men. I have stayed here too long as it is."

"I beg you to stay! I cannot stay here alone!"

"You?" cried I, under my breath. "You, who have lain here night after night alone?" and with a puzzled feeling in my brain I looked hard at her in the dim light. Could she be trying to help her men by keeping me away from mine? Yet she was not of the kind that feared anything of this sort.

She came and touched my arm.

"Please stay here by me;" she was actually pleading. Either she had suddenly changed or I had lost my wits. It could not be. Something lay beneath this.

"There is no fear in you," said I, taking her hand from my sleeve, and moving quickly to the door, and through it into the hall. I heard a stifled exclamation break from her; but my mind was made up. She had something to conceal, and, bitter at the thought, I stole softly to the head of the stairs.

But it was not to be. Even as I got to the top step a long line of light spread out from under the stairway, and, leaning over, I saw a strange sight that might well have stirred her, or any woman, or yet man, for the matter of that. The light came from an open panel beneath the stairs, and as I stood there, shooting my long nose over the rail, one — two — three — six — aye, eight — men stepped silently forth, one after the other, into the hall.

The leader, a man in a long cape coat, held a shaded lanthorn in his hand; and the others, evidently by prearranged design, spread out, each gliding silently into a room, while two, the leader and another, moved swiftly to the stairs, and began to ascend.

"So!" said I, bitterly, though in a low voice, as I stepped into the room. "So that is it, madam! You have, indeed, set me a pretty trap; and a fool like me is none too wise, but must needs fall into it. Well, mistress, I am sorry; but you shall see — "

On the instant the room became light, and I saw that she had lit the tallow dip.

"Hide here in the curtains, quick!" she whispered. "Do so quick! quick!"

'T was some instinct in me that made me glide behind the heavy curtains by the open window, as the tall cloaked figure stepped in. I could see naught, but as he entered I heard an exclamation break from him:

"So ho! my runaway wench," cried he, "and here you are in papa's old house, and in the midst of a conspiracy!"

"I know not what you mean, but I would know, sir, by what right you follow me here, and by what right you dare to come into my chamber in this fashion."

"Easily told and explained, Mistress Debby! I suspected we would run you here to earth, and so I came to find papa's daughter and bring her to her home and to her wits."

"I will do what I choose; and I do not choose to receive you, nor will you take me hence."

"Indeed, and I will, Debby! And do you make ready now in some garment fit for a horse's back, and prepare to come with me on the minute. I like not this territory. 'T is too near our rebels for comfort. And, besides, there is other work for me to do to-night."

"Leave me, sir. I have done with this, once for all!"

"You will come with me now," cried he, angrily, and stepped up to her and took her by the arm and shook her. "You will come with me now, on the instant!"

"And is there so much haste, then?"

The man wheeled on me with a suddenness that startled us all. I know not why I came forth, but I could not see her tyrannised over; and though my mind was in a whirl as to the purpose of this stranger, as well as to what might be going on below, I was out and at him with my hanger before the words were well out of his mouth.

He muttered to himself, "What the fiend is this?" as he drew and guarded my thrust. Then he cried out to his man:

"Shoot, fool! shoot him!"

Out sprang the report across the room, and a pane of glass fell behind me; but, as good luck would have it, the miss was clean and fair.

At the same time, too quick, and too tangled up with our hurrying about the room to be at first distinguished from it, came an uproar from below stairs. Shot followed shot, and we could soon hear, even above the noise we made as we thrust and parried, the sounds of fighting from beneath.

At the first he hesitated a moment, muttering,

"What may that be?" But, as I pressed him sorely, he turned to me again, crying:

"Dorkin, thou fool, fire! Waste no time! Fire, curse thy soul!"

Then I saw the man come towards me, and I knew he could not miss again. There was naught to do but run, and I ran for the great bed, followed by the leader, who had thrown his great cape back over his shoulders. As I ran I caught a chair and swung it around towards the soldier, hitting him squarely in the shins, and he bowled over, cursing with pain. That gave me a moment, and I pushed a table at my adversary; but he, catching it, swung it aside, and at it again we went.

All the while the terrible din below stairs increased, and cries and curses now added to the uproar. It ran through my mind to wonder how my men fared, and if Curtis were near enough to hear. But I could do little, for my time was near up.

"Shoot! shoot! coward," cried the man again.

I caught, out of the corner of my eye, the soldier again on his feet and walking slowly up to me, with his great pistol held before him and bearing on me. And 't is more than strange how, gone though I knew I must be, I had but one thought—she should see what a patriot could do in his last hour. So I gave a heavy lunge at my man, and again, still seeing the other growing slowly larger, — when there rang out another shot like a cannon's report in that room.

"Missed again," muttered I; but a curse from my opponent, and the heavy thud of a falling body, told me he was down. Yet did it take me long to realise what had happened; for I could not let my eye wander from the sword that flashed in front of me constantly. As we turned around one another, however, I caught the glimpse of Mistress Philipse, looking in terror at the floor in front of her, and holding my smoking revolver in her hand — and my good spirits flew back to their proper place.

Up came from below a shout, and I heard cries and steps rushing up the stairs. Still my man pressed on his work; but what I had seen her do gave me the stomach to push him to the wall. And then, too quick to be told here properly, my name sounded clear and brave in Acton's voice, accompanied by the sounds of my approaching friends. For the space of an instant we stood listening, and in that moment I turned to Mistress Philipse, and cried:

"Into the back room! quick! Wait for me there! Ah! you will attempt it, will you?" this last to my adversary, as I saw him making for the window.

'T was a hard moment's exchange of thrusts and he was too near the window; for, as I cried out and the door opened and Acton rushed in, the man turned, put his foot lightly on the low sill, and went out straight into the darkness with a fall of thrice his height below him. Yet even then, I noted that she had gone in the nick of time. All might yet be well!

We ran to the window and heard the voice of Curtis cry out, as he ran off into the night after my vanished opponent. Then I soon learned that four British soldiers were prisoners, and that five lay dead, or wounded, below. And while the men were discussing how many had escaped, Curtis walked into the room.

"Well?" said I, struck by the expression on his face.

He sat down and wiped his forehead without speaking for a moment; then said, as if to himself:

"Sometimes I almost believe in spirits."

"What now, lad?" asked Acton.

"Here was I standing in the door below," said he, rising with far more animation than he usually betrayed, "looking out into the night; when who, think ye, literally dropped from the clouds?"

"Why, lad, 't was my man jumped from the window above," said I.

Curtis shook his head.

"'T was the man with the cape! the man, as sure as I live! The man who is known to us as Hazeltine! I knew him at once. I made after him, but" — and here he shrugged his shoulders—"but he disappeared, as if the darkness had swallowed him."

And I sat down and pondered what this might mean.

CHAPTER X

WE left the house with the prisoners as quickly as possible, the dead being buried. And after continuing with the troop up the road for some distance, I turned back on the excuse of having left something.

As I came near the house again my mind misgave me. Would she wait? Would she trust me still? It would take the devil himself to tell her mind, and I could not judge. I had seen her now but three or four times, and yet I knew at least twenty different humours; and Heaven knew how many more she had at her call to do her bidding. Still, she should not have cause to doubt me. I, at least, would keep my word, and so I went on up the walk again to the side door and into the room where we had captured the maid and where the light still burned. Then on into the front hall. Listening a moment and hearing naught, I called her name.

A stifled exclamation came to me through the oak under the stairway, and the panel slid softly back. There was no light, but what worked its way across the back hall from the other room. Yet could I see her as she stepped out from the black hole, saw, too, that she leaned towards me, so that I caught her, or she had been on the floor.

What new mood was this? She was lying in my arms, her head on my shoulder, sobbing with the convulsive gasps of a child! She clung to me till the grip hurt my shoulder.

"What is it, Deborah?" I asked. "Hush! What is it? There's naught wrong now. They're gone, child!"

Yet still she sobbed on. For the life of me I could not help it — she seemed so like a child — and I patted her shoulder softly and bade her calm herself.

"I cannot! I cannot!" she sobbed. "God help me from such another hour!"

"Why, how should so brave a girl fear a dark corner?"

"Take me away! ah, wilt not take me away from here?"

"Come, now," said I, moving to the back room.

"That man!" she cried in terror, looking up into my face with a frightened gaze. "Is he gone?"

"Long since," said I, as soothingly as I might.

"Is he dead? Did I kill a man?"

"Dost know you saved my life?" I asked, holding her close. There came a convulsive grip on my shoulder again.

"Thank God! Thank God!" she murmured. "But did I kill a man?"

"No, surely not," said I. Yet the fellow lay in his new-made grave cold and stiffening fast. But she had so wild and crazed a look in her eyes I dared not add

to her terror. And 't was well I did so, for with a long
sigh the nerves relaxed, and I lifted her in my arms
and carried her out of the house into the cool morning
air and down to the road with never a word nor move
from her.

'T was a sweet burden to carry, and, as I moved
along she sighed again, in her half conscious condition,
and reaching up one round arm put it about my neck.
So could I have carried her a hundred miles. Was it
not enough to make the warm blood flow back and
forth to your heart? And would not a man give half
his days to feel such another slowly throbbing against
his coat? For the life of me I could not forbear to
take the longest way to the gate — 't was but a paltry
step at the longest.

Come to the roadside, however, and by the horses,
I sat down upon the grass and, still holding her, waited
in silence for very fear that she might wake and
force me to let her go. And then she drew something
of a long breath and opened her eyes.

" 'T is quite right here, now," said I. " We be in
the road far from the house," and she turned her head
slowly, looking up at me, her cheek touching my coat.
And I saw that the fear was gone.

" Why, where are thy nerves, girl?" I cried, with
a laugh. Could not a man laugh for very joy of life
at such a face, lying close to him, and looking up at
him so with never fear nor doubt, but oh, what a world
of trouble in the eyes? If indeed there be one who
could not, let him get him to a nunnery, for he is a
fool.

"You will not leave me?" she murmured.

"God forbid!" said I, fervently. And she moved a bit in my arms and drew another long sigh.

So I sat quiet for a space, Roger gazing down at me in wonder. And after a little she moved again.

"What is it?" said I, softly, for fear of waking her.

"I — I think I can sit up now," she answered.

"No, no," I insisted, "you're much too weak." And no doubt she was.

"I think that — that 't were better I should," said she, with a trace of herself creeping into her voice.

"Nay, child," said I again, "'t will be your certain death. Lie still!"

"Since when, sir, have you acquired the authority to command me?" she asked, yet never moving to rise. There she lay close to me, her face as pale as the moonlight, yet giving the hint of the petulant raillery in her eye and voice.

According to one, Marvin by name, I had a right to command her, and as the thought grew in my head I held her closer to me, and looked down in her eyes, and said not a word.

"Mr. Balfort!"

Aye, 't was over! There sat Mistress Deborah bolt upright beside me, taking up the tresses of her long hair with hands that might shake a little, but with no wavering in her face. Still I said not a word. Indeed, I did not like to meet her eye just then.

"I think I shall get up and walk a little," came in a constrained voice from her. And she forthwith attempted to rise. But had it not been for a quick grasp from me she would have fallen, and so, with a nervous laugh, she held to my arm again and looked up at me.

"Forgive me, dear friend! You were right. I am as weak as any nervous girl. Indeed, I am ashamed of such faintheartedness."

"Never a trace of faint heart is there about you," I answered, warmly. " But you have had a night that might well strain the nerves of a strong man. Wilt take my arm and walk?"

She looked at me searchingly and made the trial. Then on a sudden she seemed to sink from me, and grasped my arm heavily, murmuring with that strange nervous laugh in her voice:

"I am so sorry, but — but will you — would you help me to a — "

And I had my arm about her again; for, indeed, the girl could not stand.

"You are too weak to walk, and you must trust to me as a gentleman — as a friend — as a — "

" Husband?"

" I did not say so."

" You thought it, perhaps?"

" My thoughts are my own, mistress."

" Indeed, sir, I fancied they were any one's who might look on your face!"

"Does my face, then, say I am a villain?"

" O, dost not see, stupid," cried she, " how safe I feel with you out of that terrible house? Could I smile and joke, think you, after that, if I were not as free as air — only a little weak and tired and — "

And then of a sudden she leaned her head against

my shoulder and wept softly, holding my arm tight the while.

"Do not cry so, mistress! Wilt not rest quietly a moment till strength comes to you?"

"You do not understand a woman!" cried she, between sobs. "Go away and leave me — leave me alone!"

What the fiend I should do now I could not guess, till I bethought me of a pocket flask of brandy in the saddle, and, laying her quietly by the roadside, I was there and back in a moment and had forced her to take a swallow or two. After that, without more ado, I threw the reins of the two horses over one arm, and, picking her up, started down the road for the village, just as the first signs of dawn appeared over the hills.

For a time she lay quiet again, holding me tight by the shoulder; and gradually the strong liquor and her own self-control checked the quiet weeping. Thus, still lying close, she said:

"You must not carry me. 'T is too great a burden."

"I could carry you to New York and not know it."

"Am I of so little consequence, sir?"

"You are — you are — oh, child, child, you know well what you are, and how little the burden of carrying you weighs me down!" Indeed, I said it somewhat bitterly, for everything was by the ears whichever way I might look.

For answer, she moved a little, turning her face up to me.

"Where are we going?"

8

"To the village below here, where you can be warmed by a fire and have some woman to care for you."

"I need no woman to care for me," said she, quickly. "And I am quite satisfied now. But will it please your highness to let me try and walk a bit?"

Setting her down I held her while she felt her own weight, and then finding she could indeed stand, she let me lift her on Roger, and with one hand on my shoulder and the other on the good beast's neck, she rode and I walked into the village, just as the morning rays spread over the land.

"The dear sun," said she, softly. "There it is, as bright and clear as if there had been no dreadful night;" and she added presently, "It seems that we are destined to take early morning jaunts together."

I walked on in silence, still holding her arm.

"Why so silent, sir? Do you not know that my nerves need cheering up? And yet you are as glum as an owl."

"I am thinking where I should be now, if it had not been for your courage last night."

"And is your life so serious a matter as all that?"

"No, 't is not indeed. And if the fellow had touched me, little would have been missed from the world to-day."

There came a heavier grip upon my shoulder, and looking up I saw her leaning towards me with the new sunlight glistening on something in the eyes that looked earnestly down at me.

"And wilt fall morose, too, because I wept? Fie,

how weak and foolish! How like a woman!" And yet I'd be sworn 't was not that those filling eyes said to me.

"Mistress Deborah," said I, taking her hand from my shoulder, "Do you care the least how I feel? Dost know what I would say?"

"Aye, sir, you would tell me if this be not the very same village through which we passed but a few days since."

"Damn the village!" quoth I, softly, in some dudgeon.

"Sakes!" cried she, "'t is a pretty town. Why shouldst damn it, since we may yet breakfast together there — you and I, at our first meal, — you and I, the rebel chieftain and the loyal maid!"

So we rode on into the village, and, stopping at the first house of respectable look, I went in and found a good woman, who took Mistress Philipse and helped her to arrange her toilet. So I stood by the door, waiting her return, being myself, to tell the truth, worn out with the night's work and the excitement of the past few hours. I stood thus when a horseman came by from the north.

As he drew near, in spite of my own thoughts I could not forbear a smile. For he was the most comical-looking bit of humanity it had been my fortune to meet in many a day. The horse was nearer dead than alive, lanky of limb, and seeming to have more corners and angles than the famous Rosinante of the Spanish writer's Don Quixote — a fierce-looking beast with long teeth and no hair in his tail. Yet he covered the

ground, however strange his gait. But the rider
looked as he might have come from a powder magazine
that had blown him sky high and dumped him all
shattered on the earth. He wore no hat and his long
hair stood out every way but that which it was intended
it should stand, while the poor man's clothes were
ripped and torn, and hung in shreds about him. One
boot was gone, and the blood stood on his brow and
cheek, dried and black. As I say, I could not forbear
a laugh at his wild appearance; and then it dawned
on me that the man wore the shreds of a Colonial blue-
coat and cavalry uniform. Seeing me in the doorway,
he pulled up with such a suddenness that the strange
beast he rode promptly sat down. Thereupon he dis-
mounted and old Rosinante lay quietly at full length
in the road.

"What in the name of the devil have you there,
man?" cried I.

"Ye have a Colonial dress, sir," said the poor wretch
saluting, but gazing out of his bloodshot eyes suspi-
ciously. "Are ye perchance an American officer?"

I told him I was.

"Do ye, then, know aught of one, Lieutenant
Balfort, Merton Balfort?"

"Yes," said I, equally cautious. "And what of
him?"

"I have a message for him."

"I am he."

Again he looked at me.

"How am I to know?" he asked.

I thought a moment and then said: "Did you

meet any American troops going north some hours
ago?"

"Yes, sir. Cavalry, under two officers."

"These officers. Do you know their names?"

"Yes, sir."

"They were Lieutenants Curtis and Acton," said I,
"and carried British prisoners."

"Your pardon, Lieutenant," said he, humbly; and
then grasped the door-post in evident exhaustion.

"Sit down, man, and say on," said I. He sank
down on the step.

"I missed you at the fort, and came on — the road
above — I met Lieutenant Curtis — he told me you
were below at the ferry — before I got there some hell-
hound fired from the woods and killed my horse —
three of them took me — robbed me, by God, sir —
saving your presence, sir — got my despatches and
read them, and kept them — I fought them hard, sir,
but 't was no use — and then one of them hit me a
crack on the head, and — mayhap they left me for
the crows, for when I got to again, there was I by the
wayside in the bushes — and I 'm not so sure of what
I did, but remember getting a farmer to give me that
lump of clay over there, and so," with a wan smile,
"so I got on."

I picked the poor fellow up, and bade him tell me if
he knew the message or who 't was had sent it.

"I came from Tappan, sir, yesterday."

"From headquarters?" cried I.

"Aye, sir, from the General himself?"

"What was it, man? What was it?"

"'T is strange, now," he muttered, putting his hand to his head, "I heard that son of hell read it but a few hours since."

"Think, man, think!" said I, roughly.

"Yes, yes," cried he, looking up at me. "'T was an order from the Commander-in-Chief — for Lieutenant Balfort to report at headquarters at once — aye — at Tappan. Could ye, could ye give me a drink of water, sir?"

Turning to get the drink for him, I saw that Mistress Philipse had heard his message, and I would have given much to read her thoughts then.

"Well done, my man! Come, let me take you in here," and we carried him into the front room, and laid him on a sofa, and gave him his fill of water.

Then, while he lay quiet, I turned to her.

"Will you come to our breakfast?" said she, with just a shade of embarrassment in her tone, and of red on her cheek.

"Mistress," said I, "had you aught to do with the attempt to rescue André? — Nay, 't is an unfair question," I added, hurriedly, for there came a sudden change in her eyes. "I will ask another, instead. You heard this man's tale. Will — will others know of the message?"

"Does the lion eat the mouse which gnawed his bands in twain?" she asked.

"It depends upon how hungry the lion is."

"After breakfast the lion would not be so hungry."

"Then, it depends, too, on whether the lion is a chivalrous lion."

"Do you think she is?" she asked, slowly, looking out across the street.

I took her hand and kissed it gently, and said:

"I think she is. But I cannot stop for breakfast — I must be gone at once," and we moved out to the door. "What am I to do with you?"

She looked up without the shadow of a smile.

"You might sell me — or, perhaps some man would be willing to hire —"

"Madam, you jest upon a serious topic."

"Your duty bids you stay with me," said she, seriously now.

"You know I cannot."

"Is, then, Mr. Washington so much more important than your — than I?"

"'T is an unjust query. I must obey him."

"You promised to obey me until death should us part."

Was she making sport of me again?

"Wilt take me with you?" she cried impulsively.

"Will you go?" I asked, grasping her hands.

"To ride over the land together for days and days?"

"Aye, forever! Wilt go, Deborah?"

"And wouldst take a spy into Washington's very headquarters?"   ·

"And is not the lion chivalrous?" I asked again, earnestly.

"What a foolish boy," she said, softly, with a smile, giving my hand a little shake. "And yet," half to herself, "and yet I — I 'd not have you say otherwise. Nay, I stay here with good Mistress Apthorp, — 't is all arranged half an hour ago — till her husband to-morrow takes me to the Tarrytown lines. Then to home again," she added, with a sigh, "to home and the misery I tried to avoid." The quaint humour in her was all gone again, and she seemed almost to droop. An unreasoning anger got the better of me that such a condition should exist. This wretched war did naught but deprive me of — aye, of what? What, indeed? I could not for the life of me tell! Maybe much; maybe naught at all!

"Good-bye, Mistress Philipse," said I, holding out my hand.

"Good-bye, Lieutenant," said she, taking it.

And then, somehow, I drew her a little towards me and looked down into her eyes — great, brilliant eyes of brown depths. God forgive me, they were not for me, and I straightened instinctively.

Over the upturned face went a slowly rising rose colour, as she said very low:

"'T is a very weak and unhappy lion — "

"And a desperate mouse," I interrupted.

And so —

Roger went up the road under me, snorting in amazement at the extraordinary pace demanded of him.

CHAPTER XI

WE had gone but a short distance when my thoughts came trooping back, and I pulled up. I was called to Tappan — a day was lost already — and up above were men who had waylaid the messenger, who knew the contents of the note. 'T would be folly to travel back to Verplancks and give them time to take me on the road, or intercept me on the other side, if they deemed it worth their while. My feeling was that they were merely a gang of Skinners pillaging this man like all others. But they might be, too, some of the escaped squad we had outwitted in the old house, who were following up the rear of the troop. Most important of all, however, had not Curtis's ghost found me with the girl, whom he seemed to know, and would he not try to get her by taking me?

At that I turned about and made for the ferry, crossing as soon as I could and setting out at once for Tappan. I knew the road well enough; for in my two weeks at the fort I had crossed more than once, and from the drawings of the country in the colonel's possession the lay of the land was moderately clear.

,So I had moved along for a mile or more, till
Roger stopped to breathe at the peak of a long hill.
As I looked back I saw two riders some distance
behind, too far away to make them out, but 't was
evident they were coming along at a quick gait.
They seemed to have the dress of countrymen, and
on this side of the river I knew 't was not so safe
for either British or outlaw as on the other. For
a moment I hesitated, thinking to draw off the road
and let them come up and pass. Then the mission
I was on seemed too important, and the chance of
coming to blows with them too great a risk to be
taken just now. Out stretched Roger, therefore, in
his great stride, and I knew there were but few ani-
mals in the country could keep the good nag's pace.
I talked to him, as was my wont, and bade him save
himself, for that he and I had some miles to cover
and neither stumble nor slack might we indulge in.
Roger and I were friends of long standing, and
had had a run for our necks more than once. The
good beast laid back his ears, saying, as plain as if
in words, that if the devil were behind on the best
that he could bring from his sulphur home, we would
give him his due and a run for his money.

Never can a man have more exhilarating work
than such a ride with seventeen hands of splendid
horseflesh between his knees, and I laughed to myself to think of the run before us, if indeed the two
countrymen behind were in search of me.

The road lay over a rolling country — now down,
now up — now straight again, winding between passes

in the hills. So that shortly I made the top of another long climb and was about to go over a pass
between two wooded foothills, when, turning back,
I saw the two men down in the valley coming on at
the best rate their horses could carry them. At that
instant one pointed up at me, and then both urged on.
"Roger, boy, lengthen thy stride, and let them follow
till they get their fill!" And the good horse flattened
along the road in his old-time run.

Every now and then I could catch the beat of
hoofs, but they got no nearer.

I came suddenly upon a fork in the road, and met
an old oxen cart coming down one fork.

"Tell me, my man, are you for General Washington?" said I, pulling up.

"That I am, sir, God bless him!"

"Then tell me which is the way to Tappan."

"Here to the right, sir," answered he, looking at
me in some wonder.

I looked at him a moment in doubt, — then took
my chance; for such a man in such a place was like
to be on our side, in his heart, at least.

"Would you serve him, friend?"

He nodded, looking at me from his little eyes all
the while.

"Then tell two men who will come running here
in a moment that I took the other road."

"Ye'll do better to take it anyway," said he.

"Why so?" I asked sternly.

"Because I was but now stopped by a man as is
British, or I'm a Spaniard, who would know if a
man riding this way had gone by."

Again I looked the old man over.

"Ye need no' fear, sir, for you wear the uniform and I'd do what I could to help the good cause. Go on to the south'ard fork for about a mile; then turn west by a lane — there's but one — and come out on this road. If the Britisher moves no further south, ye'll be beyond him."

"God help you, old man, if you lie; but I'll take your word. Send the two down the fork after me," and Roger and I were off.

On went the nag. We reached the lane clearly enough, and I took it. Most of the way lay through the timber, and I ran out on the Tappan highway well nigh before I knew. And there, as my cursed luck would have it, stood three horsemen not five hundred yards away. They caught sight of me as I looked back at them, and we were all four off before much was thought or done.

'T was a bad business, for they had breathed a space while Roger had been covering rod after rod. Still, was I on the Tappan road and on the Tappan side of them, and had five hundred yards to the good. Even then no horse of theirs could do more than keep the distance, or mayhap work off a yard or two now and then. Giving Roger the reins on his neck, I got out my two pistols and made ready for what might come. The horse could take my guiding from the knee, and stretching out his neck he sped on.

Running up a grade and turning the top of a hill, I laughed out loud to see in the valley beneath tents and flags and all the signs of a camp, and knew that

Tappan lay but a couple of miles away. Turning in the saddle I waved my two arms at the men.

They came thundering on, and the one in the lead discharged his pistol, though it was far out of range. Looking ahead, I caught a bit of road beneath and saw the last of a troop of horse coming this way. And that gave me an idea, which the winding road suggested. Speeding on down the hill I turned a sharp corner and jumped Roger up a bank into the timber and underbrush, and then throwing my arms round his nose, held him close as the three rattled by. In a moment I was out on the highway and following after, still with the reins on the good horse's neck and a pistol in either hand.

'T was too good to be true! A fool will always spoil his own game. For I wheeled round another curve in the steep and narrow descent and came plump upon the three standing still and stopping the highway. Whether they had seen or heard the approaching troop I never knew, but four men more astonished it would be hard to find. There was not an instant to think or decide on action. I ran amongst them literally, having only sense enough to clap spur deep in Roger's flesh. 'T was a new sensation for him, for he and I never needed steel to keep us moving, and the beast leapt forward in amazement, as I fired on either side. They were no fools — those "countrymen" — for I had no more than got through when a quick report was followed by a sting in my left hand and the pistol dropped to the ground, while I wrung the arm and cursed the fiends roundly. Down

I got on the horse's neck and for an instant waited for my end.

'T is a long time, such an instant, but it had its end. Another shot sounded in the clear morning air, and I heard a howl in front and saw a horse go down as the troop came trotting around the curve. Up came Roger and wheeled about at a pressure of the knee just in time to see two of them turn about while the third lay still in the road.

No explanation was needed, but I cried out to them to take the men, and some started in pursuit, while we picked up the dead man whose coat was blackened with the fire of the powder from my close shot. And out of his pocket came a paper, that gave me a greater respect for Curtis's "ghost" than I had yet had — gave me, too, a sense of insecurity that I had not felt in that long ride.

The paper, which I read with the lieutenant who commanded the troop, was this:

"You are to cover the road to Tappan from Gowan's Ferry. Watch for a man in lieutenant's uniform, Balfort by name; get him alive if possible. But get him. Take the woman who is with him and hurt not a hair of her head. I follow the other two with the prisoners. Meet me at Gowan's Tavern to-morrow night. Wait two days there and then return.

"HAZELTINE."

"Narrow escape, Lieutenant," said the young officer.

"Indeed it was," said I, absently, and then, waking up, I told him enough of the story to persuade him to let me go on.

As I rode slowly into the camp, I began to understand the feeling Curtis had for this extraordinary man, and to feel that he knew by some strange, almost supernatural means what was going on in the American army. Yet 't was simple enough. He had taken the General's messenger, and, reading the dispatch, had sent out men to take me. Yet the thing rankled in my mind all the way to headquarters, and after, while I waited the return of General Washington.

CHAPTER XII

THE COMMANDER-IN-CHIEF

ONE, two, three hours I waited. No one knew, or would tell me, when the general might return, and though I was allowed to walk up and down the hall of the old farmhouse then used as army headquarters, or even in the road before the house, I realised that I was not out of the sight of one sentry or another during all that time. 'T was not strange, since the credentials I brought were nothing more than my word, and no one about headquarters knew my name. Noon passed and by good fortune I secured some food; and then the afternoon wore on.

In this delay I went over again the ride Roger had taken me, and harked back to Mistress Philipse's treatment of me at the Gowan's Ferry house. 'T was a marvel how that one woman could say what she chose to me, and, by such a word or look as she gave me when I left her, wipe out a hundred times the things she had charged me with but a few hours before. Could such a woman think seriously with so many moods and such sudden tempers? Could she have been serious and true in both her moods that night and this morning? I had seen her but twice and yet I knew her so well, so well. In that time she had shown me more of womanliness, of beauty, of sweetness, of

impetuous temper, of weak feminine helplessness, and
strong will, and anger than I had known in any dozen
women before. 'T was enough to turn the head of
any man, this breaking out in new expressions moment by moment, baffling beyond measure, yet com-
pelling me to forget all injustice by a single last word.

I could not get away from her now when I expected
at any moment to face the one man a soldier wishes
to be ready for, to impress favourably; and so in
the afternoon sunlight I could bring my thoughts
back to the Chief and what he might have for me to
do, only to see them sneaking back to that old mansion
by the ferry, with its open door, its dead, and its single light still burning to make it more desolate — to
the slight girlish figure travelling southward in the
company of some countryman on her way to renew
her troubles, whatever they might be.

So was I surprised by a stir about headquarters,
and, turning, saw a squad of officers approaching on
horseback, with the great unmistakable figure leading them. They passed me and entered the house
without a word, only returning salutes. None among
them did I know, except the straight figure of General Knox, whom I had seen at the Robinson house
on that fateful morning.

Shortly, however, I was summoned to enter, and
found a large low apartment occupied by the Commander-in-Chief, who was talking quietly with his
officers.

"Nay, Knox, it is a question of principle, not of
the individual. He may be, indeed, I know he is a

9

gentleman and a fine officer, but the question deals with the whole discipline of the army, not with the case of a single man."

"It is a terrible duty," replied the other, sadly shaking his head as he gazed out of the window.

The General saw me and said to the others:

"Gentlemen, I have some private business with this young man." And they went silently out of the room.

"Lieutenant Balfort," said Washington, turning to me without hesitation, "you have obeyed quickly. It is correct military discipline."

"I have been here ten hours, your Excellency."

"I know," said he. "I was, however, otherwise occupied. Lieutenant," he continued, "in such times as these, judgments must be made quickly, and they must be correct and unflinching."

I did not reply.

"I have sent for you," continued the General, "to give you a commission of great importance. I do not know you. Can I trust you?"

I looked him full in the eye, and met a glance that made me shiver in spite of myself.

"You can, sir."

"I think I can."

Then after a moment's pause: "You are not known to any one in this Hudson River country?"

"To no one but Colonel Livingstone's command."

"You are known to others."

"To others?"

"To a dozen British soldiers, five of whom are at large."

"Lieutenant Balfort," said Washington, . . . "you have obeyed quickly"

"Yes, that is true, your Excellency." How could he have heard of last night's work so soon?

"You should have taken them all. They are dangerous men, and one who escaped is more dangerous than all the dozen put together."

"It was impossible, sir, under the —"

"Nothing is impossible, young man," said Washington quietly. Then he went on, "You have never been in New York?"

"No, your Excellency."

Washington paused again.

"Lieutenant, you are to prepare to undertake a difficult work."

"Yes, your Excellency."

"You are to go to New York at once."

"Yes, your Excellency."

"You will examine the situation," he paused a moment.

"The situation of —"

"Of Benedict Arnold's house, at No. 3 Broadway. You are to form some plan for abducting the traitor Arnold across the Hudson to Communipaw, where you will be safe."

I could not reply now.

"You will then bring Arnold alive to me here." I could scarce tell where I was with this calm voice laying upon me so easily such a work.

"You can do it?"

"It shall be done, your Excellency, if the traitor is in the town."

"You will also search out a man who goes by the

name of Captain Hazeltine — ah, you know him?" for I had started involuntarily. "He may not be in the town when you get there. If not, wait for him unless the Arnold matter is more urgent."

"It shall be done, your Excellency." None might question this man.

"If you bring him to me dead or alive, you will bring the most dangerous spy in the British army. Still further: Sir Henry Clinton has by this time heard of the arrival of Rochambeau's fleet, and will be forming some plan for cutting off his co-operation with me. I must know this plan in time to stop it, or —"

"Or —"

"You must stop it yourself."

"It shall be done, your Excellency." Why I spoke with such confidence, God only knows. The whole bearing of the great soldier seemed to go into me for that moment and I felt certain all should be done as he said. I little knew what was to come.

"Lieutenant," continued Washington, still more slowly, "no human soul in this world knows of this commission but you and I, and if you are taken —"

"I shall not be, your Excellency."

"If you are taken, sir, neither I nor any human soul can save your life. You will be hung as a spy and I cannot lift a finger to help you."

"I understand," said I, looking him in the eye.

"Now, as to your necessaries," and he went into another room, returning in a moment with several papers. In the instant of his absence I had made up my mind to one thing, and as he returned, I asked:

"Your Excellency gives me three commissions?"

"Well, sir?" said he, in some surprise.

"It will be wiser to have three men execute them."

"That is impossible," he answered quickly. "Three American soldiers in New York would be discovered in an hour."

"Not the three that will go."

"It is impossible," reiterated the commander. "I am putting great reliance in my judgment when I give you these weighty commissions, but I must do it partly because the few men I have are known in New York, partly because I rely on General Putnam's recommendation of you."

"That confidence shall not be misplaced."

"I feel that it is not."

"Besides, if I fail, as you say, sir, I shall be hanged, and that will be the end of it."

"What is in your mind?" he asked, with a slow, quiet smile.

"There are two lieutenants in Colonel Livingstone's command."

Washington glanced at a bundle of papers on the table again. "Lieutenants Curtis and Acton?"

"Yes, your Excellency."

"You have known them long and well?"

"I have known them scarcely two weeks, but I know them well."

"They may betray you."

"That will be impossible."

"How is that?"

"Because I shall not tell them anything, your Excellency."

"They will go with you in ignorance?"

"They will go with me without knowing the purpose of their journey. If they succeed, they will know soon enough. If they are taken, they will die without ever knowing why they died."

"Then they are brave men."

"That they are, your Excellency," said I, earnestly. "And I beg you, sir, to let me have their assistance and counsel."

"I know one of them well, the other I have heard somewhat of. You will answer for them?"

"I will answer for them, your Excellency."

Thereupon he sat down in his chair and looked thoughtfully out of the window for a few moments. Then, collecting himself again, he opened the package of papers brought from the inner room, and, selecting two, handed them to me. They were peculiar bits of waterproof paper not more than a couple of inches by one in measurement, and as I read them carefully I could not repress an exclamation. Both were signed by Sir Henry Clinton and read as follows:

"Captain Hazeltine is to be allowed to pass and repass the British lines anywhere at any time of day or night.
"CLINTON, Commander-in-Chief."

"The bearer is on special business by my orders. He is to be allowed to pass and repass all British lines at any time with one person accompanying him.
"CLINTON, Commander-in-Chief."

Neither date nor other mark stood on these letters. How Washington could have obtained these priceless passes was, and still is, beyond me. But no one yet knows the workings of that mind and the power for details and foresight and preparation he could compass.

"Lieutenant," said he, "it would be as well for you to be dead as to have these papers found on you within our lines, for you would soon be dead thereafter."

"I shall need an order for money, and an order to Colonel Livingstone releasing Curtis and Acton, your Excellency," said I.

Again a smile played over the sad features as he said kindly:

"You have a cool head, young man. Keep it always on your shoulders. And now good-bye and good fortune!" And with the same cool self-possessed voice, after the orders were written, he signified to me that the interview was over. With a salute I went out, procured money with an order, and then went to the quarters assigned me.

Too tired to strip for sleep, I lay down and thought of the future. Hazeltine was ahead and had the powers of Clinton's army behind him. He knew us all three. Furthermore, he would do much, I knew instinctively, to take me, for that I had defeated something he had to do with Mistress Philipse. And a man who would go to the daring of sending his agents into a camp to take one, would do much to correct his mistake. I must not be known to leave Tappan, therefore, nor could Acton and Curtis be known to leave Verplancks. 'T was as plain as a pikestaff — and so I slept.

CHAPTER XIII

PROBLEM 3

'T WAS a fine cold morning that dawned after my interview with the Commander-in-Chief — a morning that will be memorable to me always as the first and only time when I became a play-actor and took on myself to play a rôle. The air had that cool, crisp feeling that tells us winter has begun to put in his finger and that soon we shall have snow. It was by far too cold at seven o'clock to be out in the open air, — at least, so thought the ferryman at Gowan's Ferry, as he betook him to the shore upon the west bank of the river to see to his boat. He was but partially awake; for, be it said under four eyes, he had not betaken himself to his rest the night before at a seasonable hour, and consequently he had slept late, which is but natural, and no doubt occurs anywhere, whether the sleeper be a ferryman at Gowan's Ferry or a king of England, or, for that matter, any one who, being human, has a regard for nature's sweet restorer.

The ferryman, upon finding his boat in readiness for whatever emergency, cast a glance over the dark, cold waters of the Hudson, rubbed first one ear and then the other, and, recording a silent hope that all others in that vicinity might have been up late the

night before and therefore sleeping late on this chilly
morning — the ferryman, I say, having allowed himself this course of reasoning in less time than it
takes to write it here, was in the act of turning towards his small house with the prospect of a short
nap between the sheets he had left cozy and warm,
when he became aware of the approach of a middle-
aged gentleman. 'T was evident even to the diluted
wits of the ferryman that his fervent prayer had
not been answered. And furthermore he realised but
too well that the gentleman, reasonably well-to-do,
mounted on his sleek, substantial horse, showed unmistakable signs of an intention to cross the Hudson.
Now this being neither agreeable nor yet amusing to
the ferryman, he became on the instant filled with unreasoning spleen, though in reality he was of the most
even and kindly disposition.

The well-to-do middle-aged gentleman on the substantial cob, you must know, was none other than
Mr. Argyle Bartlett. Mr. Bartlett was evidently
from Boston, for there was that about him which
told of the New Englander; and then, as now, most
substantial-looking middle-aged gentlemen of New
England birth hailed originally from Boston. There
was, however, something about the cut of his coat,
which, though scrupulously clean, was of a somewhat
ancient pattern, that suggested that Mr. Bartlett
might possibly have come from a town somewhat
nearer the backwoods than Boston. Mr. Bartlett
appeared to be, in other words, nothing more nor
less than a merchant of New England, who, having

set aside some profits from his business year by year, seemed now wandered somewhat far from his household gods and in no very fortunate season. And, though the ferryman did not know him from Father Adam, or from me, for that matter, he realised that he must row him across. As the traveller approached, the ferryman perceived that he had pistols in his saddle-holster and that he wore a sword. That again went to show that Mr. Argyle Bartlett was as shrewd as he was scrupulously clean, thereby exhibiting two qualities that marked him as a New Englander. "In such times," he had evidently said to himself, "in such times it is wise to go prepared for anything." Consequently he went armed.

"My good man," said Mr. Bartlett, pulling up his horse at the landing, "I would cross to the other side. I am fortunate to find you at your boat."

The ferryman, still bearing in mind the warm sheets, grew upon the instant even more untrue to his better self. He merely motioned towards the ferry and moved over to it himself. They were soon out on the river and shortly touched the eastern bank.

About noon Mr. Argyle Bartlett came up with the Verplancks pickets, and presenting his passes was taken into Colonel Livingstone's presence by the corporal of the guard. He explained his desire to be allowed to go on, stating that he was extremely pleased to be within American soldiers' protection, as he had had an uneasy time for the last five days. He carried a note from the officer in command of the American forces at Philadelphia, notifying all whom it might concern that he was Mr. Argyle Bartlett, merchant of Boston, and on his way home.

Strangers — such strangers as one might talk with — were few enough in that camp, and hence, after a short conversation as to the condition of affairs in Philadelphia, the Colonel was delighted to grant his request to be allowed to stay and have dinner with the officers. At this moment, indeed, the mess room began to fill.

Curtis and Acton, with three or four others, soon entered, and the conversation became general, though somewhat guarded; for these men had learned by long experience not to trust wholly even their own families.

As it chanced, Acton sat beside Mr. Bartlett, and they were soon talking over the South.

"I knew an Acton of Virginia, in Jamestown, long ago," said Mr. Bartlett, "a fine, tall man. But, let me see, he must be sixty — sixty-six at least now."

"Yes, there are several branches of the family there, and I had two uncles who would be that age."

"Aye, to be sure," said Mr. Bartlett. "What was Acton's first name now, — John? Nay, nay, that was not it."

"Was it Edward?"

"Yes, yes, — Edward. Indeed so 't was. 'Ted' we called him."

"Yes, he was, I know, always called 'Ted.'"

"And how is he now?"

Acton's face saddened. "He died three years ago of the fever."

"You do not tell me so!" cried Mr. Bartlett, leaning towards Acton, with that sympathy that told of
his real feelings. No one but Curtis noticed anything
beyond the ordinary in this. No eyes but the lieutenant's caught a quick movement — not even those
of Acton himself.

Then sitting back in his chair, Mr. Bartlett let his
eyes look inward and seemed to be recalling the old
times they two, Ted and he, had had together.

"Yes, yes," he continued, shaking his head sadly,
"'T is sad news to hear it. I knew him well. We
had many a hunt, he and I, in the old days, and more
than one scramble to turn the Indians off the scent
back in the fifties." Then, turning to the colonel, he
said: "There be good staunch Livingstones in the
South too, Colonel."

"Indeed there are," said that officer, "and relatives
of mine too, no doubt; but 't is many a day since I
knew of them."

And so it was natural that the talk turned on the
havoc war was making in families, in which all joined
except Curtis, who seemed averse to talking on the
subject. And then after a time Mr. Bartlett thanked
the colonel for his courtesy, wished him a speedy con-
clusion to the war, accepted a good pistol as an added
protection on his journey, and set out to strike the
North Castle road.

What followed has been told me so many times
since by my friends that I know it by heart. An
hour passed, and Acton, Curtis, the doctor, and several others were still sitting about the room. The

guard had been changed and at the moment there was naught to do. Acton sitting by the door evidently caught a draught of cool October air; for on a sudden his gaze grew fixed, his head went back and he sneezed loud enough to lift the roof. He thrust his hand into his pocket and fished out a kerchief.

"Egad, Acton, my lad," said the doctor, "ye'll have the spasms if ye repeat that. — Helloa! what's here? Aha! my friend. We've got thee now — a love-token, as I'm a sinner!" and he stooped to pick up a paper that had come from the other's pocket along with the kerchief. But the lieutenant was too quick for him.

As Acton picked it up he glanced carelessly at it and then his gaze became fixed. A puzzled look grew between his eyes, and finally he glanced at the others.

"What is 't?" asked the adjutant.

"'T is but a poor chaff, and badly done at that!"

"Well, man, what is 't? Read it!" said several.

Curtis was smoking quietly some distance away, but he turned to listen as Acton said:

"A sorry hit, as I'm a sinner."

"But what have ye there, man," said the doctor. "Read it out and let us hear the hit."

Acton then read slowly the following:

"Problem 3.

"A can ride to Hardcastle in four hours at six miles an hour by the shorter road. B can do it in three hours at eight miles an hour on the same road, starting earlier. How far must C go by the longer road if he travels six hours and goes at the rate represented by the sum of one half the rate of each of the others, and when must he start in order to arrive one hour after A?"

No one could keep back a smile at the puzzled expression on the lieutenant's face as he read this simple problem, that is to say, no one except Curtis; and, as he got up with the others to look at the paper, his face took on a thoughtful look that passed unnoticed at the moment.

"Oh, lad, you cannot hoodwink us," laughed the adjutant. "You 're trying to coach yourself in the rule of three."

"Keep it up," cried the doctor, "and ye 'll come out first in the class," and thereupon every one laughed.

At that the lieutenant grew a bit vexed, which was as near as he ever came to anger.

"Well, 't is a weak skid," he muttered. "And I hope ye like the look of it, Rob," he added, as Curtis took the sheet of paper and examined it carefully.

"O, aye," said the other, carelessly, "'t is paper, no doubt. Keep it, man, and study out the answer."

"Not I," cried Acton, and, crumbling it up, he threw it under the table and stalked out. The others followed on different duties, but Curtis remained, smiling thoughtfully. In a few moments he reached under the table, picked up the paper, smoothed it out, and studied it with an amount of care that would have set an observer thinking. Then, carefully folding it, he put it into his pocket and went in search of his friend.

He found him walking along the river bank.

"John, my lad," said he, "you're very tough in the skull."

Acton, colouring hotly, turned upon him.

"Where are thy wits, man?" said Curtis. Acton said not a word, as they walked slowly from the camp. When they were in the open fields and well out of hearing, Curtis took out the paper containing "Problem 3" and held it towards his friend.

"Now, John, read it again."

"I tell thee, Curtis, thou'rt ridiculing me, and 't is not to be borne."

"I was never more serious in my life."

"But 't is all nonsense!"

"'T is naught of the kind."

"Well," said the other, trying to smile, in order to keep himself from growing vexed again, "give it me," and he read it again.

"Now solve it."

"Rob, 't is unfair in you to carry the thing to such lengths."

"'T is you that are unfair, my friend," answered the other, seriously enough.

"Why I can answer it in a moment. So — 4 times 6 is 24, 3 times 8 is — "

"John Acton," said Curtis, pulling up in his walk and facing his friend, "what is thy name?"

"Come, lad, let it drop!" said the other in an altered tone, "lest I lose my temper."

"Thy name, man!"

"Acton!" roared the lieutenant, now actually irritated.

"What does it begin with?"

"A! but I will not —"

"What is our friend's name who left us a few days ago?"

Acton looked at the other a moment and then said slowly:

"Balfort."

"And his name begins —"

"With B."

"And my name —"

"Is Curtis and begins with C," said Acton, pulling a long face and looking at the paper in his hand.

"Now read 'Problem 3' again," said Curtis, "putting in the names."

Acton began:

"Acton can ride to Hardcastle —"

"Which might be," interrupted the other, "without much change —"

"North Castle," muttered Acton. "Acton can ride to North Castle in four hours at six miles an hour by the shorter road. Balfort can do it in three hours at eight miles an hour on the same road, starting earlier —"

"Which he has already done," put in Curtis.

"How far must Curtis go by the longer road, if he travels six hours and goes at the rate represented by the sum of one half the rate of each of the others, and when should he start, in order to arrive half an hour after Acton?"

The men looked at one another with the two different expressions of countenance that may well be imagined.

I've thought often since how I would like to have seen them then. Finally, Acton gasped:

"Rob, I am indeed an idiot."

"'T is precisely what I said," answered the other, drily.

"Then we meet Balfort at North Castle."

"Certainly."

"And you go by the lower and I by the upper road."

"Precisely."

"And you are to get there half an hour after me."

"Exactly." Curtis's replies were the pith of dryness.

"And you are to start an hour and a half after me."

"Correct again."

"Then we shall not be noticed leaving here nor arriving there."

"Ye grow sagacious, my friend."

"'T is not only idiocy; 't is nigh upon stupidity!"

"Which I presumed to suggest but a moment ago," replied the lieutenant.

"But wilt tell me, then, how, in heaven's name, the thing came into my pocket?"

"Aye, now, that 's it! How think ye?"

Acton said not a word.

"Was it there before lunch?"

"Let me see, — no! it could not have been. I set that kerchief in my pocket just as we started for the mess."

"Didst sit by any one at lunch, perhaps?" asked Curtis, blandly.

"Aye! I sat — Rob! Rob! ye would not tell me — ye do not mean — that Mr. Argyle Bartlett, merchant of Boston, was Merton Balfort?"

"At last," said Curtis, casting his eyes heavenward.

"Well, may I be damned!" exclaimed Acton.

"Nay," answered the other, laughing, "rather be ready to go by the upper road to North Castle in four hours."

"But this must be serious, if such care is necessary."

"Still more, it would seem important that no American soldier should know of it."

"And how do we get leave to go?"

"There you have me," replied Curtis. "'T is the one thing that catches me. Yet if Balfort finds it necessary to go to this length to insure secrecy, you may say surely he has arranged in some way for our absence. So let us go back, get ready, and — wait." Upon which they returned to the barracks.

Acton was on the point of putting together a few necessaries for the journey, when an orderly entered and reported that Colonel Livingstone would see him at headquarters at once. He smiled as he thought of what perplexity he might have been in if Curtis had not cleared the way. Passing by his friend's quarters, he stepped in and found him quietly smoking.

"I have my summons already," said he softly.

"And I must be at headquarters at five this afternoon," replied the other.

"Decidedly the thing is serious."

"Decidedly."

By half after five Curtis had passed the pickets to the south.

By seven Acton took the upper road and started his horse at a six mile gait for North Castle. And it seemed as if no one in the world knew anything of all this, but General Washington in Tappan and the two men themselves besides Colonel Livingstone. Yet things are not always as they seem.

CHAPTER XIV

NORTH CASTLE was hardly a village in 1780, for it consisted of but a cluster of houses along one road. Yet did it boast a general supply store, and was proud in the possession of a house for travellers known as Holt's Tavern. This house was no different from any other in the town, except that perhaps it was a bit larger, and that it had a sign swinging before the main door. 'T was older, too, than many of the other habitations in the village, and the slightly projecting upper stories witnessed that it had been built when the fear of Indians had been greater than the fear of Tories to-day. This projection of the upper story was not more than a foot, but if, as you entered by the front door, you cast a look upward, there might you see holes at regular intervals which pierced the small projection. They were stuffed now with paper to keep out the cold; but there had been a time when our fathers had stood in the upper chambers and fired good shots through these same openings, sending many a treacherous Indian to his own happy or unhappy hunting-ground.

Within, the house consisted, on the ground floor, of a hall running through to the back. On either side were moderately large rooms, and at the back of the

Holt's Tavern

hall was a small flight of steps going up to the second story, which in turn was divided into four or five rooms.

To the right of the door, in the large room, burned now, at eleven of the night, a large wood fire. Tables stood here and there, and at the back ran a bench, or bar, behind which sat a fat old woman knitting on a high stool, so that she might sew and still keep her bulging eye on all that took place within the chamber. By the fire sat two men whom I rightly guessed to be American soldiers, and in the corner, by a table, occupied in eating an evening meal, which the officious innkeeper, bustling about the room, had put before me, sat my wearied self, more anxious than I would have confessed, waiting for the two friends, the fear growing on me that dear old Acton would never think to look in his pocket nor comprehend the message when he did. I had thought to leave it with Curtis, but, no opportunity offering, I was forced to take Acton as the means, and just before going I had left the General's release for the two lieutenants at the colonel's headquarters. 'T was an anxious two hours, only brought to a close by the entrance of John Acton in civilian's dress. He knew me at once, for Mr. Argyle Bartlett was safely stowed away in the woods back on the roadside, tied up in a bundle of his own clothes.

I feared at first that the honest fellow would come up to me and blurt out the whole thing, but, as I afterwards learned, Curtis had given him the best of lessons in the, to him, quite unknown art of deception. Thus he stepped into the room, ordered a mug of are and, like myself, took a pipe and some tobacco, and, sitting himself near me, looked what he doubtless was — the picture of uneasiness and discontent.

While the two soldiers talked quietly by the fire, I turned to him and asked:

"Have you come from the westward?"

"Aye, from the river."

"Have you heard what is to become of André?"

"No, there was naught given out when I left."

At the mention of André the two soldiers by the fire stopped their conversation, and one of them, turning toward the table, said:

"He was taken from here day before yesterday."

"Is 't known where he is confined?" I asked. The landlord here put in his oar, and ventured:

"They do say as they took him to Tappan for trial."

"Ah, no, Holt, 't is not likely so," said the soldier. "He went up to West Point, I am sure."

"We cannot say a word here," said I, in a low voice, in Acton's ear at this moment. "And yet must I talk with you as soon as Curtis arrives."

"Well, but would he not go that way sure?" asked the tavern-keeper. "They 'd be afeared of a rescue down below."

"Can't we go outside?" whispered Acton. Lord forgive him! his whispers were like the rumbling of thunder.

"Outside!" exclaimed the soldier, "what is there to go outside of?"

Acton looked confused.

"This gentleman refers to the frigate *Vulture*, which

has been lying off Teller's Point. Doubtless he is right, and mayhap the escort was instructed to keep well outside the reach of her guns."

" O, aye, 't is likely so," said the soldier, " for I have heard she lies there."

I caught Acton on the point of saying something to wreck the whole business, and had just given him a jab beneath the table when the door opened. Every one turned to see who else might be arriving at this late hour, and I could not help a silent curse at the luck to see two strange men enter, nod to the tavern-keeper, and walk over to the fire.

" A cold night, sirs," said one of the new-comers.

" Aye, the year 's moving on," answered the big-voiced soldier.

" Bad! bad!" said I, softly, " but we must wait for him."

Acton nodded. Meanwhile the new-comers ordered a cold supper, the landlord having nothing else, and sat them down by the table near us. They had scarcely settled to their meal when again the door opened and Curtis entered. Even the tavern-keeper looked surprised to see such a company so late; but a poke from his matter-of-fact wife sent him about his business. Curtis had changed his uniform and was dressed like any well-to-do young New Yorker in knee breeches of snuff colour, top-boots, a double-breasted waistcoat, with a frilled shirt and a long buff coat. He threw off a riding-coat and discovered his pistols and a long hanger.

The calm, serious face was as composed as usual,

nor did the man disturb himself to look at any one in particular, but took the seat assigned to him near the rest of us. One of the strangers spoke to Acton after a moment.

"You say that you have come from the westward, sir. Did you find the road free from traffic?"

"I met not a soul from the time I left the river."

"We two are bound westward, and 't is said the road to Gowan's Ferry is full of these wild Skinners and cowboys."

"I can answer for that road," volunteered Curtis. "Not a soul is stirring to-night, for I have but just come over it."

Meantime I had caught Curtis's eye and by an almost imperceptible movement saw the same thought in his mind that was working in mine. These two men coming from the east had a suspicious manner. Neither of us could have said just why at that moment, but by this glance we both agreed to watch them. The meal went on and in a few moments the two strangers lit their pipes and went over to the fire. Curtis was still eating.

"What are we to do?" I asked under my breath.

"Wait," said Curtis in the same voice, and then he added aloud: "Master — er — "

"Holt, sir, at your bidding, sir," said the landlord, trying to bend his fat belly in a bow and rubbing his hands together.

"Master Holt, can you give me a room to-night?"

"Well, yes, gentlemen," said the tavern-keeper effusively. "Certainly, certainly. I suppose, now, these

two gentlemen," pointing to the two men from the
east, " will have a room by themselves — a large room
't is, at that, sir, and I can give you three gentlemen
accommodation easily. Of course, in these times, sirs,
perhaps two will never mind being together. We keep
a fine tavern, sirs, none such another the whole country round, and my madam, she — "

The landlord stopped abruptly and turned around,
for the door at the back of the room opened and a
little shaver ran up to him and was now tugging at
his coat. The host stopped and listened to what the
boy had to say. Then out rang a howl from him, and
he turned a clay colour:

" My God! Oh! oh! sirs, we shall all be killed! "
and he wrung his hands.

" What is 't, Holt, man? What 's to do? " cried the
two soldiers.

" Oh, Lord! Oh! they 're here again! they 've been
here before. I know 'em. They know I have a little
set by for my old age! I 'm ruined! I 'm ruined! "
and the tears rolled down his cheeks.

At this moment the woman shrieked from behind
the counter, and we knew that the wife had the news
as well. Every one had arisen and was standing,
when such an interruption at this moment so bewildered and maddened me that I cried out:

" Well, man, what in the devil's name ails thee?
Speak up! "

" The Skinners! the Skinners! They 're coming to
rob me," screamed the terrified tavern-keeper.

" In that case," said the calm voice of Curtis,

" 't would not be amiss to drop that bar across the front door and pull the shutters to."

Evidently the landlord had a little sense left, for in a bound he was at the door and had the huge iron bar in its place between two iron staples. At the same moment one of the two soldiers stepped to the front window to close the wooden shutters. His head had scarcely passed through the frame when a loud report came to us from outside, and the poor fellow rolled back and fell upon the floor, shot clean through the head.

'T was quite enough to break the spell that hung over us. Every one was talking and running to blockade windows with tables and chairs, for most men of those days had had some training in such scenes before now. Curtis, Acton, and I naturally drew together, and as we thrust a table against a window, another shot came through it, and a pounding began on the door.

" 'T is bad, bad!" I muttered.

" On the contrary," said Curtis, " nothing could be more fortunate."

" I do not see it in that light," answered I, testily. " We shall be separated without having talked."

" On the contrary, again, my friend, we can now talk without fear of interruption; while before we should have been hard put to it to find a way."

Another shot came through the table and clipped a bit off the shoulder of Acton's coat.

" But we shall be killed, and then our expedition will fail," cried I.

"Nay, nay," said Acton, "Rob has the right of it. We need have no fear of interruption now. We can —"

"Master Holt, turn out the light," cried I sharply, "then they cannot see." Out went the light instantly. Outside every noise ceased as if by magic.

"Well, how shall we talk?" muttered I, for it seemed the last straw — this untimely attack.

"Hold thy tongue, man, and I'll show thee," said Curtis. "Holt," he continued, "and you, sirs, come over this way. So, now landlord, you are attacked, I see."

"Attacked? My God, I'm ruined. I'm a dead man —"

"That you will be, if you do not act."

"But what can I do?"

"Have you guns?"

"Aye, three."

"Very well; do you, your wife and this remaining soldier with the boy go upstairs with two of the guns and fire down on these men from above."

"We can fire through the old loop-holes," said his wife.

"Good, so much the better. These two men and myself will take the ground floor front and kill any one who tries to enter. The two gentlemen who have just eaten with us will guard the rear of the house."

"But I —"

A crash now sounded in the hall.

"The door! the door!" cried the landlord and his wife in one voice.

"You see, there is no time to lose," said the cold, clear voice of Curtis. Indeed, the coolness of the man and the reason in all he said made us instinctively put ourselves under his command, and in a few moments the two strangers were in the kitchen, watching the rear door, the tavern-keeper and his wife with the boy and the soldier were upstairs; and we three were barricading the weakened door by a device of Curtis's, which consisted of a huge table wedged between the door and a projection of the chimney that went up on one side of the narrow hall.

"Now, my friends," said Curtis coolly, in his natural voice, when the door was strengthened, "let us sit here between the hall and the main room and hear what Balfort has to say."

CHAPTER XV

BUT it is very uncertain if we can get out of here alive," said I, irritated in some way by this excessive calmness of Curtis and the jovial ease of Mr. John Acton.

"My dear lad," said Curtis, "you asked for a place where we could talk without fear of interruption. I give you one. I can do no more. Doubtless this is a band of Skinners of not more than six or seven, and could not we three hold this house against twenty?"

"Then, look you, Balfort," urged Acton, "we shall have the satisfaction of knocking some one on the head. I owe these fellows a debt. Nay, 't is a stroke of luck they are come."

At this moment the report of a musket rang out overhead, and a heavy weight fell against the outside of the door near which we sat. A deep groan was followed by a moment of silence.

"Aha! you skunk," cried a voice from the hall above, "that for the shot you gave my brother." The voice was scarcely stilled when a fusillade sounded from across the road and several bullets struck the stout oak of the door.

" Seven," muttered I to myself.

" Seven what?" asked Acton.

" There are eight in that party and one is dead. You are right, Curtis, 't is indeed better than I thought. We can handle seven. I feared there were more."

" Stay, but I do not see — "

" My dear John," laughed Curtis, "mayhap you did not notice that seven bullets pelted the house but now."

" First of all," said I, checking some other remark of Acton's, "before I give you my work — did you notice the two men who ate at our table?"

" Oh, aye, they were natives, sure enough."

" Right, lad, but they hail from New York," said Curtis slowly.

" From New York?" cried Acton.

" Precisely," said I. " But they have just now come from Boston or near there."

" Balfort, my friend, you are better than I," said Curtis, smiling in the darkness; "how know you that?"

" Their boots and clothes are covered with mud. It has not rained to the westward in ten days. They have come from the east, therefore, where I hear it has rained for several days."

" Man, you are a genius!" cried Acton.

" Furthermore," said I, "the mud is light in colour and sandy, whereas hereabouts 't is red and dirty. 'T is sandy only near the seacoast."

" How do you know they hail from New York?" persisted Acton.

" S-s-st," whispered Curtis. All three sat in the darkness. Nothing could be heard for a moment and then the unmistakable crackling of a twig sounded through the window of the main room. Curtis crept towards the window with pistol in hand. There was a bit of opening where the table failed to cover the window, and, placing his eye to this, he saw the dim outline of a figure crawling around the corner of the house. Softly, coolly, he put the pistol to the opening, took a slow aim and fired, dropping immediately to the floor himself. There was no sound or movement in the grass, but the next instant a bullet came diagonally through the small opening and flattened itself against the doorpost above my head.

" Did you get him?" asked John.

" The attacking party now consists of six," replied Curtis.

" And now as to our instructions," said Acton.

" We are to go to New York to accomplish three things, which I may not tell you till we be there."

" Very well," said Acton, " we are to go to New York; that is sufficient. What next?"

" We go separately and meet there. That is, one goes alone and the other two together. I have passes for one and for two travelling in company. Once there, I can tell you in good earnest there is much to do. But here looms up the question as to where we shall meet there and be unobserved."

" I have been in the town," said Acton, promptly. " Let us meet at the village of Greenwich and go into the town together."

"So far good," said I, "but we must have some base to work from, — some spot to meet in. Curtis, what think you?"

For a moment during this bit of discussion Curtis had said not a word. Now, though I could not see his face, for the darkness, I got an instinctive idea that something was wrong. In fact, after once seeing Acton pulled up when he tried to question his friend about something to do with an event of several years ago, I had made up my mind to steer clear of any references, so far as Rob Curtis was concerned, beyond the limits of camp life. Before I spoke, 't was clear to me that something was amiss. The moment he answered the change in his voice was so great, yet so quiet, that I started, as did Acton, almost persuaded that some other sat by us in the gloomy smoking hall.

"Balfort," said he, slowly, "is it of grave importance that we should go into New York?"

I did not reply at once. I was too struck with the change and all that such a change must mean in such a man.

"You shall judge for yourself. I am commissioned," and I leaned over close to the other two, "I am commissioned by General Washington himself alone. No other knows aught of the thing but you two. 'T is not even to be written down. I am to go to New York to do three things, one is no more than a piece of daring; the other two are of the gravest importance. One, if accomplished, may save hundreds — thousands of lives."

"And these you may not tell to us?" asked Curtis, still in that low voice.

"No, friend, not till we are on the ground."

"'T is better so," said the same deep, sonorous voice so unlike his. "We can be of no use to them as prisoners."

"These commissions are not for one man to carry out. I therefore asked for you two and obtained your release."

"And you did well," said Curtis.

"Well, well, Rob, did I not say as much ten minutes gone?" cried Acton, impatiently. "There stands no doubt or question; but where are we to meet?"

"Where in the town must we go?" asked Curtis, still pursuing his own course.

"All over the town, but especially at No. 3 Broadway."

There were two shots overhead at this moment, and it may have been for this reason that Curtis started so suddenly. He made no reply at once, but when he did he said:

"Impress this on your memory — No. 2 Broadway."

"No. 2 Broadway," said we together.

"Well, we are to meet there."

"You know the place?" I asked.

"Yes."

"You know New York, then?" said I, incautiously.

"My friend," said Curtis, "a moment ago you asked us to accompany you to New York to help you at the risk of our lives, and told us we were not to know the reason —"

11

"And, my dear friend," said I, "neither Acton nor I will ask why or how you can help us."

"No. 2 Broadway, then, let it be. Now as to getting there — but I think something is happening in the next room."

As Curtis spoke, a shot had been fired from the kitchen, and now came another report from outside, and with it a long, low cry from the house. Almost immediately some one yelled "Fire! fire!" and ran into the hall. We stood an instant, and then, happening to be nearest, I ran through the tap-room and thrust open the kitchen door. A bright light shining in the room, I had started towards the fire when I was checked by the cry of a man immediately in front of me. Another step, and I had fallen over him.

"Here, John!" cried the wounded man, "I'm hit bad. John, I cannot see you. Take the papers and get out of here. They must be delivered! Where are you?" cried the man again, for the other had run into the next room in search of water for the fire. "The papers, John," cried the dying man again, "in the back — part — of my — shirt. Clinton must have them — to-morrow. Take 'em — sure — I —" He had tried to sit up, but now fell over into my arms.

I took a belt knife and ripped up the back of the man's coat, tearing off the greater part of the garment to make a wad for his head. 'T was scarcely done when the other came back to the room, now brightly lighted by the burning of the window-sash, and he and Curtis and Acton ripped off the boards of the window. A shot or two came into the room, but each man looked to it that he was not in range. Then of a sudden the stranger turned towards his companion and caught my eye as I bent over him.

"He is quite dead," said I, as the other approached; "shot through the head."

"Let me see," said he, quickly, and, pushing me aside, he began feeling of the man, going through each and every one of his pockets, muttering the while to himself.

"The fire, man!" cried I. "Let him be now; he is better off than we." Then the tavern-keeper appeared, bringing water-pails, and the stranger took one.

"Holt!" said Curtis; "stay here and we will return to the front of the house. 'T is two to one they take this opportunity to attack there." And so we started for the front again.

And as we did so there came another crack and the moonlight shot in through a fracture in the big oak door. A man's head appeared, and Acton, grasping a chair, held it in front of him, and, leaping on the table, rammed it against the head, forcing the man back with a roar of pain. Then, standing still on the table but not in front of the hole, Acton began to converse with the unknown outside.

"Now, gentlemen," said he gaily, "the first head that shows itself will get scalped."

"Surrender!" cried two or three gruff voices.

"Ready, ready, step up, gentlemen! one at a time, to be scalped!" cried the imperturbable Acton.

"Surrender, you there, and we'll give you quarter,

if you turn the house over to us!" said a gruff voice again.

"No use to surrender, my dears," replied Acton, "because the house is already turned over to the flames."

"Then we 'll shoot every soul of you!" cried another voice.

"Shoot away, but do stick thy addled pate through and get scalped!"

There was a short conference outside and then the Skinners drew out of ear and gun shot.

"Now to finish our arrangements," said Curtis, coolly.

"Aye, and in quick order, too, for the house is burning down," and in truth I was in some concern.

"Well, we meet as soon as possible at No. 2 Broadway," said Acton.

"Just so," replied I. "Curtis, you know New York?"

"I do."

"Then take this pass and come to No. 2 as soon as possible. Acton and I go together."

"But what is No. 2? How are we to get in?" asked Acton.

"True, that is important," said I. "What shall we say, Curtis?"

He hesitated a moment. In the meantime we could hear the crackling of the flames mingled with the cries of the inmates of the house. Finally he said slowly:

"You will find an old woman there."

"An old woman," we repeated.

"Tell her you have come to meet Robert."

"We are to meet Robert."

"And, my friends, if you have any regard for me, question her not at all; but do as you say — wait for me."

Now came Madam Holt rushing in, crying that the house was falling about our ears. Behind her was her crazed husband.

"Holt, you say you have money here," said Curtis.

"I? I, money? no, not a cent, as the good God knows!" screamed the frantic man.

"Fear not, man! Go and fetch it and we will make a sortie and charge through these men. There be but five of them now."

"Oh, my house! my house! I'm dead! I'm ruined!" cried the distracted man, clapping his hands to his head as he hurried away.

"One word more," said Curtis. "That man who was killed in the other room is one of the two we suspect. Mayhap he carried despatches."

"He did," said I.

"Then we may and must get them," said Curtis.

"I have the papers here," and I held them up.

"Balfort," cried Acton, as the landlord came rushing again into the now lighted room, "ye are certainly a great man!"

"And now," continued Curtis, as we moved toward the door, "each man save himself; Acton with you, and I alone; and we meet at No. 2." We went from the main room into the hall and found it thick with smoke. All were there however, huddled together, the tavern-keeper, his wife, the boy, the soldier, but the surviving messenger was gone. And then several discharges of musketry rang out in the night air.

" 'T is the end of him and like to be of us soon," said the soldier grimly.

" End of whom? " asked the trembling landlord.

" That Yankee that was with the man that 's dead in there. He bolted for the woods."

" Maybe he is dead, and maybe not," said I. " Be that as it may, we are not dead yet. Master Holt, how far are the woods from the rear of the house?"

" Not a hundred yards," said the wife, her husband being too paralysed with fear to reply.

" Set fire to the chairs in the front room to attract the Skinners there. Then to the woods and the village with all of us!"

Another discharge of musketry sounded on the night air and we heard a cheer. The soldier jumped to the front door and gave a loud whistle by placing his finger to his mouth. There was a reply in an instant, and at the same time a rapid scattering fire rang out along the road.

" 'T is over, friends!" cried the soldier. " Here be the troop come back in the nick of time."

" Now is our time, then," said I, quietly, to Acton; and as the others went to the front rooms, we bolted from the smoky hall, through the burning kitchen, to the woods.

Curtis had remained behind.

CHAPTER XVI

A CASE OF MISTAKEN IDENTITY

IT was but an hour after sunrise, clear and warm
— an Indian summer morning, if ever there was
one — when we turned out of the North Castle
road into the main highway of the Hudson, and, as
I judged, not far above Tarrytown. The darkness,
the weariness of the long ride, and the nervous strain
of the night and the attack on the tavern had kept us
both silent for a long time. Only now and then would
Acton come out with some joke, or laugh at the tavern-
keeper's money bag, or the terrified look that took them
all when we got the news of the coming attack.
Nothing ever seemed — nay, nothing has ever, to my
knowledge, seemed to make the least difference in this
man's peace of mind. The great healthy fellow knew
not what melancholy or weariness meant. But I was
weighed down with the work ahead of us, the memory
— now always with me — of that one face, and the
weariness of my sleepless nights.

With the bright rising sun, however, and the beginning of as beautiful a day as one could pray for, we
brightened up a bit. Acton spoke up after a space of
deep thought that seemed to weigh his great shoulders
with its importance, and I gathered from his first word
the drift of his trouble. Indeed, the thing had been in
my mind all through the night.

"How think you, Balfort, Rob comes to know so much of New York?"

"I have wondered myself, friend. You have known him well?"

"Aye, for two long years."

"'T is strange, his knowing so surely a house in the very midst of British headquarters," I murmured, half thinking aloud.

"You have an unworthy thought there, my friend," said the big fellow in a stiff voice. "Is not Rob going with ye, and no questions asked, though he risk his life?"

"Nay, nay, Acton. 'T is not suspicion of the man. But you cannot guess the importance of the mission. Suppose — suppose we should miscarry for any reason!"

The lad pulled his horse up in the middle of the road, and looking at me with a flashing eye said:

"Balfort, Rob Curtis is my tried friend. No such thing may be said of him to me. So that I can leave you and return to him."

"Tut! tut! man," cried I. "You 're wrong. I do not suspect him. I am but struck with this extraordinary thing that I do not understand."

"And did he question you?"

'T was well hit home.

"I do not comprehend it myself, but I know my friend and that is enough," he went on, moving along again, but none too graciously. I had hurt the honest soul.

"Enough for me, too," said I — and then my hand

flew to my head, for on the instant my hat flew off, and there rang out the ping of a rifle.

"Ho, ho!" roared Acton. "Here he is! Here in the woods!" and he turned his horse to ride up the bank into the underbrush.

"Stop, you fool!" cried I. "Down! down in the saddle and ride!"

"But I must find this —"

"Ride, ride!" I cried, again. "There's no time for delay now!"

Another shot passed us without harm, as I got my horse to a run, and Acton came after more slowly, sitting bolt upright in the saddle, while he growled out his disgust at this cowardly retreat. Yet could we hear the clatter of hoofs behind; and turning, I saw half a dozen men, suddenly appearing on the road, and coming after.

"Our horses are done up. They will overtake us in a mile," I said, thinking aloud.

"So! so!" jeered the man. "We will take two as they come on, ride two more down by force and that leaves but one apiece to finish the game. 'T is too simple."

"'T is no such thing," cried I, nervously, as we sped along. "We cannot risk delay. Spur on, lad! spur on!" for a shot sped over our heads. "They are in range now," and I turned to take a look at them. And then I called out suddenly.

"What is it?" he asked, turning too, in the saddle.

"Look at the first man, look, John!"

"Damnation!" said he. "Curtis's man!"

"Aye! aye!" said I, "Captain Hazeltine, as I'm a sinner. The man is the devil himself!"

I thought for a moment my companion would then and there pull up, but I, begging him for the work we had to do to ride on, he did so; and, abruptly turning a bend in the road, we saw there two hundred yards ahead, a platoon of redcoats presenting arms. We had reached the British outposts above Tarrytown.

"My! my!" said Acton in his sarcastic raillery, "here is a sandwich that will be hard on the digestion!"

But there came then into my head an idea, and we sped on directly into them, waving our hands backwards as the six pursuers turned the bend.

"Get them all!" I cried in a tone of command, as the sergeant in charge ordered his men to prepare to fire, bewildered though he was at our sudden appearance. Yet, seeing two men rushing confidently into his arms, pursued by six others, he naturally enough, and as I had hoped, took the pursuers for the enemy.

A sharp volley rang out as the six came on without checking, and the result was extraordinary. The leading horse leaped into the air, fell heavily forward, turning a complete somersault, and threw his rider head foremost into the road, where he lay still. One of the five fell heavily from his horse, and the others wheeled as if at drill and rushed back around the bend, evidently having had enough of their view of the post.

Turning to the sergeant, I said:

"I thank you for your timely assistance. Those cowboys would have made short work of us."

"There be many of them hereabouts," said he, politely, though he still had a bewildered look in his face.

"We were coming down from the eastward and found these men in ambush," I continued, without giving him time to think overmuch, "and —"

"And the big chap let out at us. He's a spy of some kind, I know —" the stupid Acton began, but to cut his dangerous talk short I interrupted:

"Doubtless you would know who we are," as some of the soldiers proceeded to pick up the two fallen men.

"'T will be necessary. Will ye come to the lieutenant?"

In an old house by the road that had been taken for a guard-house, we found the lieutenant commanding. I began on him at once:

"My name is Hazeltine, sir, and I am on my way to New York with despatches for Sir Henry Clinton. My companion here is included in these passes," and I handed him Washington's priceless gift. He had but begun to glance over this when the door opened and Hazeltine himself entered. His face was a mass of blood and dirt, but beneath this you could see the features working with a well-nigh ungovernable passion. He threw off the sergeant without an effort and strode directly up to the officer.

"You are a new officer here, sir. Otherwise you would know me."

Acton began to prepare himself for anything that might happen. I stood where I was, trying to appear only annoyed at this interruption. The officer, on his part, instead of replying, turned to his sergeant and blurted out:

"Why do ye admit this man here?"

"Lord, sir, he came of his own accord, sir," answered the man.

"Well, have we not force enough here to put one man under guard? Take him away!"

"Lieutenant, you will regret any such action," cried Hazeltine, angrily.

"Why, you outlaw, do you expect to impose on me?"

"I tell you, sir, Sir Henry Clinton will not appreciate such summary measures. I come here to tell you my name is Hazeltine, and I say to you 'rebellious war'! — aha, you will give attention now, eh?"

The lieutenant started perceptibly twice during these hastily spoken words, once at the name of Hazeltine and once at the words "rebellious war."

'T was high time something was said, and so I took the cue:

"I know this man, lieutenant, and you will do well to hold him. He is an American spy in disguise. I nearly caught him a few days ago at Gowan's Tavern just above here in the neutral country."

"You lie, you dog! You lie!" cried the other. "I know you now, too. You are the rebel I am after, and so is this fellow here. You — What have you done with —"

"Silence!" cried the lieutenant, "and leave the questions to me! Now, sir," he continued, turning to me, "proceed."

"I tell you that my name is Hazeltine and that —"

"He lies! he lies! That is my name!" cried the man.

I shrugged my shoulders as quietly as might be, and looked at the lieutenant. Acton began to laugh. He was beginning to comprehend. The lieutenant was fast losing all comprehension.

"Will ye be quiet!" roared he at the stranger. Receiving no answer he turned again to me.

"Now, sir!"

"I repeat, my name is Hazeltine, and if you will give me a few moments' private conversation, I will prove it. I may not expose important matters here."

"You will answer here, sir, what questions are put to you!" cried the lieutenant, fast losing his senses. "Now, then," he continued, sitting down to the table, and beginning to write, "your name?"

"Paul Hazeltine."

A movement on the part of the blood-bespattered man drew a corresponding movement from the lieutenant, and I put my hand to my hip. Of a surety the situation looked critical. Acton alone appeared calm, and a smile gradually spread over his great face. There was the prospect of a fracas, and therefore of amusement. Consequently he was the coolest of the party.

"Your business here within the lines?" continued the lieutenant.

"Special emissary of Sir Henry Clinton. If you will allow me a few moments' private conversation —"

"I will allow ye naught, sir, but the guard-house,

if ye do not reply at once," cried the bewildered officer.

"Here is my pass," said I, handing him Washington's slip. Then, as for an instant there was silence, the door again opened and two soldiers brought in the other man, who had been wounded in the head in his fall from his horse. Acton touched me quietly, and turning I saw 't was the man who had escaped from Holt's Tavern the night before, and who had failed to find the despatches on his friend's body before he left. His head was bandaged, but he was not to be mistaken.

"Who the hell is this one?" cried the lieutenant.

The sergeant touched his hat and replied:

"The other Skinner, sir, hit in the head, sir. He's out of the game, I'm thinking." Lieutenant Majoribanks bent over him and at that moment the man opened his eyes and struggled to a sitting position. I have never become accustomed to death, much of the grim customer as I have seen, and the struggles of this poor fellow to say something that was on his mind were pitiful.

"What is it?" asked the lieutenant, leaning over him, the anger gone out of his face and voice; "try again, my man!"

We all instinctively kept silence in the sight of the fast approaching end, and I heard the one word "despatches" as he pointed at me. 'T was a close hit, but by the grace of a chance thought I found Hazeltine in line with me and just behind, and turned and looked at him.

"Despatches," repeated the poor fellow. "That —
man — my — despatches!" And over he went with
a thump of his head against the floor as dead as was
ever any man.

The officer rose in a moment and turned to us. Seeing me look at Hazeltine, he said:

"What does this mean? You have despatches?"

"Not I," said Hazeltine, his manner changing a
shade as he spoke. I held my peace for a moment, for
the eyes of the officer showed that the mistaken iden-
tity was working into his head, and I have ever found
that a bit of silence at certain moments will say more
than years of wordy converse.

"Not I," repeated Hazeltine. "He pointed to this
man here. I know him well. He —"

"Sergeant," ordered the officer, "take this man
into custody. Search him and bring all papers found
on him to me!"

Again Hazeltine controlled his temper by a great
effort. Indeed, the man's mind was working fast, and
I knew from what the Commander-in-Chief had told
me that he had a brain of great power.

"Lieutenant," he said between his teeth, "'t is as
good as the loss of your commission to touch me.
Will you do it, or will you give me fifteen minutes?"

The officer looked at him a moment with a deep
frown on his face, and then turned about and cried:

"Well, sergeant, do I give you orders twice?"

It was quite enough. Hazeltine was down in an
instant, struggle as he might, and bound hand and foot.
He looked at me with as evil a colour in his red eye

as one might call up in a bad dream, but said not a
word; and then out came from his coat a package of
papers. The lieutenant looked them over.

"Take him away to the guard-house and bring me
anything else you find," he ordered; and they carried
the man out, still with his red eye on me till the door
closed behind them. And thus I knew that until one
of us should be dead that man Hazeltine was my
enemy, king or no king, war or no war, and 't is not
in me to deny that it was an ugly sword to hang over
one by day and night.

I do not mind a fair fight in the light of day, but
God defend me from the vicious hatred of a fiend such
as this man showed himself to be in that one look. The
courtesy with which the officer of the post conferred
with me about the papers, after I had shown him at
his order what I carried, and the kindness with which
he then sped us on our way with fresh horses, re-
questing me to take Hazeltine's despatches with me,
did not carry off the cold feeling that had settled somewhere in the pit of my stomach at the man's look.

However, we were in well guarded territory now,
and passed post after post on our ride into the city.
At Greenwich we stopped a moment for the last outpost examination, and then rode on down by the
water's side through a muddy road over the creek
and into the town.

'T was a dusky, foggy night with signs of rain and
a high wind that sent darkness and light over the
slimy street in quick succession as the clouds swept
by the moon. I had little time to notice much, but at

the top of the town we passed on the left a long row
of buildings that I knew must be the great barracks.

Further on were the ruins of a beautiful church on
the right, that I knew, too, must be Trinity Church,
burned in the great fire a few years before. It lay
close by the old wall of the town, now fallen into dis-
use, and we met many people groping along here and
there in the mud and a crowd of carriages interspersed
with a chariot or two. Once we must needs wait a
few moments till a line of vehicles could move on,
and one of the chariots brought back to my mind a
certain wet country road and such another vehicle
tilted over to one side with the face of a young girl
looking out of its windows at me.

"What the devil means this crowd?" said I.

"Crowd, man!" said Acton, "why, do you not
know you are in a city, my friend? And that just
below here Clinton holds a court as high and mighty
as George the Third at Windsor? Where, think ye,
are ye, then; in camp?"

"Then we are near No. 2 Broadway?" I asked.

"Aye, here we are," he answered as we came opposite the head of the line of carriages, which were
discharging ladies with silken gowns and powdered
wigs at a covered bit of canvas that hung over the
door of the great house. The place was lit from top
to bottom, and I could hear fiddles jigging out a dance
amidst the hum of a hundred voices, jocose greetings
of men, and yells of servants in livery crying out to
one coachman to move on and to another to move up.
'T was a bustling and brilliant scene out there in the

dimly lighted, filthy street. For no light, except what came from a lanthorn here and there over a door, or escaped from the great house, served to give the eye the smallest chance.

"Beyond a doubt that is the house, and he holds court this very night," said Acton, as we came opposite the entrance with the line of carriages between us and the door. 'T was a jam, indeed, and before we knew it, we were caught between two lines of cursing coachmen, one driving up to the door, the other turning and moving back.

A chariot drew up, and I had leaned down on my horse's neck to look through the windows up the steps and into the house, when the vicious hiss of a whip on the other side sent my beast, that was none of the best, by a side jump against the coach, bringing me up to the door with a thump that shook the whole vehicle. And then I had like to have fallen into the mud; for there, looking at me out of the window, in some white and silken gown, with a whiter neck peeping out from under a furry cape, was a face I had had by me these ten days.

She knew me on the instant, and started forward with a cry of surprise, as if to speak. And then, on the impulse, the powdered head went up with a movement I knew full well, and the stare that only a high-bred woman knows how to call up from some depth within her met my eye, as a gruff voice behind her cried:

"Have a care there, my man! What the devil, would you ride in here by us? Come, Deborah, we are at the door," and I was pulled on by the frightened horse and reached the door across the street, I know not how, in a daze of mind that finally landed me in a ditch by the gutter, as I slid off his back.

She had known me, I would swear; and yet she had given me as cold a denial as ever heartless wench gave any man. And yet, — 't was but human nature to think it, — yet I had saved more than her life but a fortnight ago, and risked my own skin in the saving. But what should I, Merton Balfort, expect, after all, and what right had I to think it could or should be otherwise?

Still, what tricks the mind will play! I knew then that that face had been by me ever since the night at the old tavern, and in my foolish thoughts the next meeting had happened again and again; but the reality was of a far different order from the dream.

CHAPTER XVII

AS I looked about me to gather a bit of the situation of the house, I could not forbear an exclamation; for, dark as it was, I could see but a sorry house for our abode. The building was a straight affair, narrow and high, with a pointed roof like a Dutch house, and, though at first the house appeared to be complete, I saw in a moment that it had been practically destroyed by fire. The lower rooms seemed to be hastily repaired, but the upper windows had no frames or glass in them, and the whole was blackened with singed wood.

Back of the house and towards the water I could make out in the murky darkness the black ruins of burned dwellings, and here and there tents built over roofless rooms, with now and then a light shining through the slits in the cloth.

Acton was standing grumbling to himself as was his wont.

"This is no place for us," said he; "we shall be caught in a hole like rats."

"The longer we stand here, the more likely," I answered, and forthwith rapped upon the door with my sword-hilt. No reply coming, we pushed in the door, and, it giving easily to our weight, we entered to find a long, narrow hall, and stairs running straight up towards the next story. At the farther end a light showed beneath a door, and with a step we were at it, finding, on opening, an old woman confronting us with wonder and suspicion in her silent face.

"Who be ye, then?" asked she, after a moment.

"Listen, woman," said I, quickly, "speak not so loud. We come here from Robert — from Robert, you understand," I added, as I saw her face go white and eager, "and we are to wait here secretly for him —"

"Him?" cried she, under her breath. "You will not let him come here? He must not now! 'T would be his death! How came ye to let him come?"

"He comes of his own accord, and sent us on before," said I. "Do not fear for him! He can watch over his own safety without our aid. But instead, give us food and drink, if you have it."

She looked at us doubtfully a moment, and then went into the back room which appeared to be the one chamber in the house spared by the fire. In a few moments we sat down to a dish of salt beef and bread. I then carefully opened the despatches found on the dead man, and discovered them to be a full account of the forces at and around Newport, detailing Rochambeau's strength and the number of militia troops furnished him by Rhode Island, Connecticut, and Massachusetts, though to my certain knowledge the number was understated.

Following out a plan I had thought up, I altered

the figures by scratching those given and writing in between the lines more than three times the number above, as had already been done in one or two cases. The despatches of Hazeltine were letters from Major André written in prison, and a statement giving out that Washington was about to make an attack on Paulus Hook and Staten Island, with some description of the plan of attack. Whether this were true or not, I could not tell, but I must take my chance. We were in the act of sealing up the packets again, when there came a thundering pounding on the outer door.

"What is it?" cried the woman.

"Open in the name of the king!" cried a voice from the outside.

"Oho!" said Acton under his moustache. "They call upon us soon, eh?" and he drew his sword and stood looking at me.

"Quick, woman," I said, "go to the door, and do you do the talking."

"What shall I say?"

"Ask who it is and what's wanted."

This she did, we standing by her close to the door.

"Open in the name of the king!" cried the deep voice again, "or we will break down the door!"

Acton and I stood back, silent in the darkness, with a stiff problem ahead of us, for there was no mistaking the voice of Hazeltine.

"Well, will you open?" cried the voice a third time, and then I bade Acton, more by signs than anything else, stand by the handle of the door.

"When I open, catch him and bring him in," I whispered, "and put in all the strength in your big body."

He nodded, and at my whispered instruction the woman said again:

"What for? Why should I open?"

"Because I have a warrant for the arrest of a man now in this house."

"There's none here," she answered, and then, as I told her, cried out: "The door sticks. You must push from the outside."

There came a muffled oath, and then a savage kick at the door, and I heard other voices.

"Harder," cried the old woman, who seemed to grasp the idea, and as I felt a body press against the door, I let it swing suddenly open, and a man was driven into the hall and the door shut again before he realised that he was down and one of the strongest men in the Colonies sitting on him with his fingers so tight upon his gullet that he could only gurgle softly. We had him in the other room bound and gagged in a moment, but the pounding on the door was enough to wake the town.

"Open in the name of the king!" cried a dozen voices, and then the old door, strong as it had been made, gave perceptibly to the force from without. I turned to the woman.

"Is there a back way out?"

"Only into the lane, thence to Beaver Street in among the ruins; but ye can go upstairs and down the outside steps at the back."

"So be it, and quick, too! Acton, pick up your
man and come on." We were upstairs, had laid him
in the gable, and were hurrying down to the second
story again, when a crash told us we were too late,
and in a moment the hall was full of men. They saw
us at the top of the stairs, and started up.

"Now, man, let them have it," I cried, and we both
fired at the leaders as they came up two steps at a
time. Two men threw up their arms and fell back
on the others and the whole crew rolled back to the
floor.

"Again, Acton."

"Aye, man," laughed the reckless chap, "take the
first, and I the second. So! we wasted nothing."
Four men lay dead on the stairs before the others
could retreat. But our four pistols were of no further use.

I am no fool to lose heart in a tight place, but the
game seemed up as we saw them gather together for
another charge.

"Yield yourselves, and we'll do ye no harm," cried
one. "If ye do not, God help your souls!"

"Don't bother strangers by calling on 'em," said
Acton, in a jeering tone, "but come on, my lambs,
and take us!"

A growl was the only answer as they started up
the stairs again. We had the slight advantage of
light, as well as of being above, and as the first two
began to engage Acton, who stood at the top, I
knocked the nearest over with the butt of my pistol,
and then, leaning out from the crazy balustrade, be-

gan an exchange of thrusts with the next two, they
fighting straight over their heads, I down upon them.

They stood their ground well, preventing by their
own bodies any others from taking part, until another
jeering laugh from Acton was followed by the bodies
of his men tumbling back upon them, tripping the
whole crew over one another to the bottom, amid
cries and curses that would have raised the dead.
The howl was taken up by those in the hall and then
to our consternation a loud shout of many voices came
from the street. Running to the sashless window, I
saw half a hundred soldiers crowded around the
door.

"Back again!" cried Acton, "the town's on the
way upstairs!" and in truth it looked so; for they
had found a round table, and holding this above and
before them, they were coming slowly up two abreast
and as close as they could step.

"I have it," cried Acton — the man seemed always
to become gay in a fight and find his best wits at the
most hopeless time. "Quick, man, that cupboard!
'T will make cheese of the whole lot." And we lifted
a great double-doored clothes-press standing in the
hall, Acton, the woman, and I, and pushed it over the
stairs, carrying balustrade and all with it. The blow
was a terrible one, for the weight of the cupboard
carried the table down upon the eight or ten men and
all went down together, amid dust and cries and roars
of laughter from Acton that fairly set me off as well.

The situation was changed for the moment, for the
brave cupboard had jammed itself in the stairway

preventing any ascent or descent by that passage for some good minutes to come. In the pause that followed, a stifled cry from the old woman showed us behind the spot where the cupboard had stood a frameless window looking out on the roof of the next house. Roof there was none, however, — only blackened timbers, with here and there a patch of shingles still clinging in place.

'T was a chance, and we took it. We were out in a moment, clambering over the creaking timbers and down on the farther side into a lane, no wider than a man's body, between two buildings. There was but one way to go, and that into Broadway, and in another moment we were at the back of the crowd of two or three hundred people standing about the door of the fated No. 2, howling and yelling, asking questions and giving opinions to one another. Manifestly this was the safest place for the moment, till we heard a cry of joy from the inside, and knew that the leaders must have overcome our friendly cupboard.

"Come," said I to Acton, and led him across the green to Clinton's house, easily distinguishable for its many lights and the music coming from it. At the door we were challenged by a sentry and asked what was our business.

"Special message to the Commander-in-Chief. I must see him at once," said I, looking at Acton in fear that the absolute astonishment sitting on his face would end the matter then and there.

"You cannot see him now, man. He is —"

" 'T is a dangerous thing to waste time, my friend,

when Sir Henry Clinton is concerned. Call his secretary here at once," and I stood aside on the steps to
allow some late arrivals to enter, as if the matter were
settled.

"But you 'll get us hanged, man," whispered Acton,
"if you —"

"Hold thy tongue, man!" I said in the same tone.

"But I don't see —"

"Well, corporal, are you not gone yet?" I asked,
angrily. "Do you know that your head will drop off,
if this delay gets about?"

"I have my doubts," he answered; "but I 'll call
Mr. Cameron."

Cameron, then, was the secretary, and he came in
a moment, dressed in black and rubbing his thin hands
together.

"Mr. Cameron," I said before he could speak, "I
am Mr. Merton, and this is Mr. Roberts. We have
just come from Newport and Verplancks with despatches for Sir Henry. Will you notify him at
once?" And I showed him the despatches.

He looked at us a moment through his narrow little
eyes, and finally said:

"Come this way, gentlemen, if you please," and,
going around the side of the house, we entered by a
smaller door into a cross corridor. As we passed
along, I saw a brilliant series of rooms, polished floors,
and groups of uniformed men and beautifully dressed
women walking up and down the hall and dancing in
the large ball-room. Then in an instant we stood in
a dimly-lighted room.

At the end of five minutes a large door opened on the other side of the study or office, and a bright light from one of the ball-rooms burst in upon us. A large hand held the door for an instant, and my body stiffened as I heard a lively girlish voice I knew in my dreams now, saying half angrily, half playfully:

"But, Sir Henry, this is my dance!"

"My dear Mistress Debby, I am far more unhappy about it than you can be," said a high, somewhat querulous masculine voice.

"I do not believe it! If 't were true, you would not run away so."

There came some answer, which was lost to us in the study; for at that moment the door opened wide, and a tall, thick-set man entered, and closed it quickly behind him. He stood still a moment, not being able to distinguish clearly in the dark room.

Sir Henry Clinton at that period was well advanced in years. He would have been a handsome man but for his eyes, which by their expression gave to his face a sinister look that became more marked as he spoke. He had only left his home in England that he might win fame for himself in a few short months and return with a great name to his native land. His ill-success against the American army, and his utter inability to cope with a mind like my Commander-in-Chief's had increased this dissatisfied, querulous, complaining side of his character, and he had now become thoroughly disgusted with the whole war. Such had been the gossip of this commander of the British forces in America which had reached the ears of all of us out in Connecticut. Everywhere his troops would win battles according to European methods, and then be forced to retreat, losing more men in the retreat than the Americans had in the fight. This was anything but encouraging; and the general showed his chronic pettishness in his every action. He showed it now, as he said sharply:

"Well, Cameron, are you there?"

"Yes, your Excellency."

"Well, well, man! Speak up! 'T is doubtless something of importance that causes you to call me now!"

"I think it is, your Excellency. Here is a messenger from Boston and Newport!"

"Ah, I see him now. Well, sir, what is it?"

I handed him the despatches taken from the dead soldier. As he glanced over the papers, he rang a bell, and bade the orderly who appeared to search out and bring to him Lord Howe.

"And, orderly — !" he added.

"Yes, your Excellency."

"Speak to the general cautiously, and bring him away without attracting attention."

"Yes, your Excellency."

Nothing further was said until Lord Howe appeared.

Howe had been superseded in the command of the American forces of the British army by Clinton, and for that reason alone he bore the present commander no very good will. But, beside this, he knew perfectly well that he was the abler officer. He was anxious, therefore, to be recalled to England to avoid

association as an inferior with Clinton. In the meantime, anything that made his rival's position more
difficult only gave him the greater satisfaction.

"My lord," said Sir Henry. "Mr. —"

"Merton," I prompted.

"Mr. Merton, here, has just arrived with news that
a French fleet is lying in Newport Harbour waiting
to co-operate with the rebels!"

Lord Howe had just come from a dance, and was
very warm. He wiped his forehead and then replied
calmly:

"'T is the same as our news of several days ago,
Sir Henry. What strength have they?"

I stepped forward to prevent questions coming to
me, and said:

"I have further news!"

"What, still more?" cried Sir Henry. "This seems
enough for one night!"

"Major André has been taken to Tappan and he
is to be tried there as a spy immediately."

"What is the sentiment as to the result?" asked
Howe.

"That he will be hung," I answered.

"Then will I hang every solitary American in
New York, whether loyal or rebel!" cried Sir Henry,
stamping his foot, while tears of vexation came into
his eyes. "Do you at once take measures —"

"Pardon me, Sir Henry," interrupted Lord Howe,
coldly; "will you permit me to take some steps in
this matter?"

"By all means. I wash my hands of it!"

"Mr. Merton," said Howe, turning to me.

"Yes, sir."

"Remain in the house for an hour. If you receive no instructions within that time, call here at eight o'clock each morning until you do. Is that correct, Sir Henry?" he asked.

Clinton was evidently terribly affected by the news of André's sentence, and could not turn his mind to anything else. He said with an effort:

"Mr. Merton, you have not eaten, probably. Go in and join the ball and eat to your satisfaction. My lord, I am too stricken with grief to join my guests. Will you take these gentlemen in and make my excuses?"

Lord Howe turned, and, at my attempting to apologise because of our costumes, he bade Cameron have us brushed up, and insisted upon my putting on a coat and waistcoat of Sir Henry's, the one faced with red, the other of white satin. Acton was a sight when he was ready. He was always a handsome, great fellow; but dressed in these colours he would be noticed anywhere, and with the combined expression of absolute ignorance of the situation and his usual careless fearlessness he would have brought me to laughter, if I had not had a great fear of what he might do.

So we left the study through the door by which Clinton had entered, and found ourselves the next moment in the most brilliant scene that had yet met my Puritan eyes. I have no doubt the court at Windsor, or Whitehall, was finer, but I had heard

for more than a year that Clinton held here a magnificent court of his own, which vied, so our reports
told, even with the king's. In the great ball-room
the lights of hundreds of candles, hanging from the
ceilings in groups, and all about the walls, lit up
and reflected in the polished floor a hundred or more
gay red uniforms, with here and there a blue or
black German officer's dress, and the white and pink
and blue silks of women whose fair shoulders and
necks held as high heads and as beautiful faces as I
could imagine.

Some danced gracefully a minuet, or the waltz.
Others sat about in beautiful mahogany furniture,
and still others stood in groups talking and laughing as if no war, nor misery, nor any suffering
troops were on the surface of the earth, to say
nothing of all this at their very door. I could not
understand it. After all, 't was a besieged town, and
the frightful small-pox was raging all about them,
and still I could see one beauty after another flirting
with her fan and her bright eyes with some tall
Britisher, and gossiping of the scandal of the hour
as the fiddlers drew out the slow measures of a waltz.

Up to such a group we now came, and Lord
Howe, with no very good grace, accosted an old
woman, with wrinkled cheeks and a scrawny neck,
yet bedecked in silks and satins, and with a towering
headdress that made her bob about like a decrepit
peacock.

"Madam De Lancy," said he, bowing low, "permit me to present Mr. Merton, who has just arrived."

The old lady looked at me through her lorgnettes with a vicious squint:

"Mr. Merton," said she. "What Merton? Anything to do with the Mertons of Salem?"

"The same family, ma'am," said I, truthfully enough, yet I could not see what business it might perchance be of hers.

"A bad lot," she continued, taking down her newfangled eye-glass; "traitors to their king, most of them, except Edward, — and he has fled, they say."

I have never, God knows, had the control of my too vigorous temper, and it will even to this day get the better of me at precisely the wrong moment, even as now when I must needs answer somewhat briskly:

"Such division of sentiment is not confined to one family, ma'am, in these days."

The result of this, bad taste as it was, was like to have upset me; for the old dame turned purple in the face and gripped her fan as she cried:

"What business is that of yours, sir?"

I was on the point of answering something to turn her unexplained wrath when I caught the sound of a particular kind of stifled gasp that had something so familiar in it as to make me turn about — and find myself face to face with Deborah Philipse. Yet I should scarce have known her. Her hair was up from her face, powdered and with a flower in it, and her dress was of some light silken cloth, I know not of what colour or quality, so made as to show her fair young neck and shoulders, then running down to her waist in some sort of a pointed bodice all covered with a flowery design.

She was beautiful! She would be beautiful in the most wretched dress that was ever cast off by beggar! She would be beautiful anywhere! But now, in such a gown as I had never seen, she was as lovely a specimen of young womanhood as stood in that room, or any room this side of heaven — aye, perhaps, on the other side, too. But I knew her eyes and her voice when she said with fine sarcasm, as she might to a stranger who had insulted her:

"You deal in generalities, sir. 'T is bad taste."

I could not hold her look, and so let my eyes fall, and shuffled my feet in awkward fashion. Lord Howe saved me.

"One must know the niece nowadays as well as the aunt, eh, ma'am? Mistress Philipse, I have the honour to present Mr. Merton," and he bowed with a reverence and a look that I did not like. What was she to him, I wonder? In my turn I bowed and apologised, I know not what, to Madam De Lancy, and then in a moment I had been presented, as well as Acton, to several ladies and one or two officers, — Major Sproat, Mistress Knyphausen, General Patterson, and other young men and women. Howe then moved away, saying:

"Mr. Merton and his friend have ridden far and eaten nothing, and by Sir Henry's orders he is to be fed. Mistress Debby, will you act as commissariat?"

But Acton I saw with many misgivings already striding across the polished floor, laughing and talking with the little minx, Mistress Knyphausen. What would the reckless fool say? I hated to have him out of my reach.

"Well, Sir Starved Man," said the young lady at my elbow, "will you eat? I must obey my orders."

I offered her my arm, and bowing to the group we went into the banquet room across the hall, and when I had procured some food of a nature that was absolutely unknown to me — something of truffles and spices, and sandwiches with paste of I know not what substance in them — she led me without a word into the side hall and sat down upon the lower steps of the stairway.

"So, sir," she began in another tone, "I know now who you are. It seems that you enjoy the profession of a spy." I turned on her and looked her well in the face. "Do you not think, perchance, that you might take a hint from Major André's situation that may work so ill for him?"

"Madam," said I, "if I could equal André as a man, I would be willing to belong to what you are pleased to call his profession. He was the type of a gentleman."

"*Was?*" she asked, under her breath.

"He is dead, Mistress Philipse, or will be in a few days," I said, gently.

"André has been — been —"

"He was condemned two days ago."

"It is terrible, terrible," and she looked at me with sorrow in her eyes. "Why do you stoop to such things?"

"I am not such a man! I am not a spy, and
what I do now is neither your affair nor mine. I
serve one who must be obeyed, and I do what he tells
me to do. 'T is no more enjoyable a work than the
one I had to do a few days ago." I know not why
I spoke so bitterly. Perhaps because I had not till
that moment looked upon myself as doing the work
indeed of a veritable spy. "You have me in your
power, mistress, and you can to-night put an end to
another spy, as you are pleased to infer I am. I
cannot prevent you. Indeed, I do not know that I
care to."

She looked at me intently for some moments and
then glancing beyond me murmured:

"I do not know. I cannot tell. Perhaps I should,
for I believe I know the reason for your presence
here, and it is no doubt my duty — yes, indeed,
I have been there," she cried, suddenly, in a
lively voice. " 'T is a pretty town, Boston, but so
prayerful."

I looked at her in amazement, and then heard over
my shoulder:

"Debby, 't is long past midnight. We must go
home."

She sat quietly a moment, and I rose and bowed to
Judge Philipse, her father — a dignified and courtly
grey-haired man of sixty, in a kind of court dress,
I suppose, with long faced coat and knee-breeches.

"I will come directly, papa," she said. "Mr. Merton is just here from a journey, and Lord Howe
has bidden me see that he eats."

The Baroness Riedesel

He bowed without a word and moved on.

"I do not know what I should do," she continued.

"The tables are turned, Mistress Deborah," said I. "My life is in your hands," and I saw her look quickly at me with a serious depth in her eyes. Then that glint came on a sudden, and she murmured:

"Very well, then, you will do exactly as I bid, or — or suffer the consequences!"

"I must."

"Then accept the invitation you will receive in a moment for to-morrow night."

"I can do naught but my duty, and that occupies me."

"Oh, you cannot? We will see. I shall take my course as you select." Then in an instant she was looking at me earnestly. "Do it for me! I want to tell you of something," and she got up and walked towards a lady of graceful figure and as sweet and sincere a face as I had yet seen in that gay room.

"Mr. Merton, let me present you to the dearest woman in this whole world, the Baroness Riedesel."

With an amused laugh the lady gave me her hand, and I bent over it without affectation, for any one could see that she was a generous, loving woman with a heart big enough for all, and a face that was as beautiful as it was good. She spoke with a marked accent, but in perfect English.

"I am very glad to know Mr. Merton."

"But that is not all," said the brazen young woman at my side, "I want you to do something very kind to me."

"What is it, Debby, dear?" asked the baroness.

"Ask him to your supper to-morrow night. I find I knew him once long, long ago in Boston. Will you, dear?"

The older lady leaned over and kissed her, laughing.

"Surely. Will you come at six, Mr. Merton? We live next the corner of Wall and William Streets, close by Governor Tryon's mansion."

I said I would, and thanked her, and we moved on to find the girl's father. As we approached, she looked up at me with a bland and child-like expression, and said softly:

"You may live a day longer, sir!" and was gone.

I saw a cluster of young men in uniforms gather about her and beseech a dance, and heard them tell her she had driven Sir Henry away by her actions. And then she was the centre of the room, with the men around her like bees, talking and laughing as if she had not another thought in the world, and I knew it was right so, for was there another head set so jauntily on such another pair of shoulders in all that room?

I stood, saying over to myself again and again, "Yet she is my wife, young coxcomb that art leading her away so proudly! She is my wife, man! She is my wife!" And I went out through the hall saying it under my breath, and found Acton and took him off, saying it over and over again, till he began asking me what the devil ailed me, and what I muttered about, and had I noticed Mistress This and Mistress That, and I bade him go hang himself for a dirty spy as he was.

CHAPTER XVIII

THE DINNER OF THE BARONESS RIEDESEL

AT the stroke of six the next night I stood before the fine mansion which the Baroness Riedesel occupied, with a foreboding, and, to tell good truth, a bit of a fluttering in my insides. We, Acton and I, had late in the night slipped back into the ruined house and found the old woman lying in the back room nearly dead with terror, and with the mark of a foul blow over her eye and down her cheek. We got her up and brought her to, only to find Hazeltine gone. 'T was no place for us, and so, on her advice, and deeming the open method wisest, we betook ourselves to the "Star and Garter," a boarding-house kept by Mrs. Hodges at the Battery, down below Clinton's mansion and over against old Fort George.

There we stayed all day, working out, partly from our window view, partly from our information, the lay of the land back of Arnold's house, just above the Commander-in-Chief's mansion. Only once I went out to find a man named Low, who had been mentioned to me as a brave patriot of the Sons of Liberty, living under the stigma of Toryism to serve his country by staying in the city — a doctor-chirurgeon. I went down Wall Street, by the hosts of shops that had laces and silks and satins in their windows, and rare fruits, and met ladies daintily picking their way from carriages through the muddy streets, full of pitfalls and holes and filthy gutters where the drains ran.

Four times in that hour I met carts with canvases over them, but not so completely as to prevent one from seeing half a dozen dead bodies lying one on the other beneath the covering, going, so a shop-keeper told me, to the trenches up above the city, where they were thrown to rot in the sun and rain. Many of them were my compatriots, who had lain in the Sugar House or Bridewell Prison, — for many thousands of our poor fellows lay here still, since the day, more than three years ago, when I had marched north with Putnam for my life. Low I found at last, and a good man and true he was to me. Somehow he knew of my coming, and we arranged a plan for an attack at the foot of Arnold's garden two days hence.

Then I left Acton, telling him — more shame be it to me — that I was going to sup in order that I might get word of Arnold's habits. And yet what came of that dinner would have made me stop a bit, had I foreseen it. And so I was ushered into the drawing-room in the finest coat and breeks I could buy in the shops and a tie and lace front that made me feel like a gaudy popinjay from some sickly European court. The baroness came in a moment and kindly bade me sit, saying the others would be there in a few moments. Indeed I found the custom prevailed to arrive half an hour late, which seemed to me then, and does still, to be a foolish bit of inane fashion.

"Do you know," said she, with genuine tears in her eyes, "that we have just heard of our friend Major André's horrible sentence. Did you know him, Mr. Merton?"

"I never saw him, but he was a good and true gentleman," I answered.

"These are terrible days. I cannot sleep o' nights for thinking that my little daughters may catch this terrible plague. Only this afternoon my husband told me that twenty-seven of the poor prisoners died of it yesterday on the prison ships in the harbour. I wish I might do something to aid them, but, beautiful as our house is, we have hard labour to get wood and food, such is the price of all necessaries."

My better self warmed to the lady and I told her she had a good heart, and that I, too, could not keep my thoughts from the wretched prisoners.

"Governor Tryon and General Patterson, the commandant of the town, are goodness itself to me," said she. "But 't is a terrible time and often I yearn and long for my own dear Brunswick."

"'T is indeed a terrible time, ma'am, but if all the women had but such hearts as yours the suffering would be infinitely less."

She gave me a smile, though there were tears in her eyes, and held out her hand to me.

"We can do so little, and dare not attempt an opinion," she said.

I stooped over her white fingers and kissed them, just as some one entered the room. Looking up, I caught a glance from a pair of dark eyes that sent a thrill of joy through my body, and made me laugh in spite of myself; for there stood Mistress Philipse with as surprised a pout on her pretty lips as ever was seen. Did she think I was paying court to another? God be thanked, if she did!

But there was no time for more than a greeting and a friendly kiss from the hostess, when in came the governor of the town, Tryon, with his wife and daughter, Major Sproat, a Lieutenant Purdy, General Patterson, and a man they called Captain Atherton, who seemed to me at the moment to look strangely familiar. Then, as we sat about the room, I made note that every one rose, and turning to the door saw a young man, hardly more than a boy, enter, talking easily with his companion and nodding here and there as he walked over to the baroness, and I guessed rightly that 't was the young Prince Henry, whose coming had reached even our Connecticut ears. Finally, with much fuss of chariot and horses outside, up drove the decrepit old peacock, Madam De Lancy.

"And why should I not be out?" cried she in a venomous voice to the host, who had but congratulated himself on her being there. "Do you think I am too old to get out of my bed?"

"*Gott verbar*, ma'am," cried the baron. "You grow younger every day."

"'T is a wonder I live at all. Can you not give

us a stick of wood to cook by, major?" cried she, turning on Sproat who stood near. "Here have I to-day paid eight pound for a pitiful cord."

"Ma'am," said the major, with apology in his tone, "we are every hour sending parties to Long Island to get it as best they can."

"Stuff and nonsense," cried the old dame, her face twitching like a play-actor's. "Why do ye not cut down the trees out here in the street? I wish the rebels were all gone to the devil!" and she hobbled off on the arm of an officer to a beautiful mahogany chair that never was made in our land.

We were now a goodly company of twenty at least, and, supper being announced by a factotum all powdered like the rest, I stood at one side till the baroness passing me said, "Go and take in Deborah." Then, looking at me with a friendly smile, but a sad face, "Be good and kind to her to-night, for she is in a great trouble."

Trouble? What could be the trouble, I thought, as I passed over to her and gave her my arm?

There was some difficulty in getting the proper place in line, for each officer must go in as his rank dictated, and so, led by the young prince and the baroness, we marched into the banquet room with swish of silken gowns and tinkle of spurred boots.

After the saying of a grace, all were talking at the long table at once and the murmur of voices kept me from hearing many words, except those on either side and immediately next to me. And, indeed, the dishes that loaded the board and were each moment

set before us by five or six men-servants were by a
good half unknown to me. Beef I could tell, and
a dish of chicken, but there were others built up
high with pasty and mixed in with coloured sauces,
the like of which I had not seen before.

Blessed with a good appetite, I tasted all the men
passed to me and found them palatable. Talk ran
on current things, of the recent fight in Staten Island,
of André's coming execution, and anything that came
up; until, in the midst of a foolish remark of her
own invention and with a laugh on her face, I heard
Mistress Philipse saying in a low voice, as if it came
from some one else:

"I have much to say to you — two things. Have
a care of your countenance and let no one read in
your face what you hear."

For a moment I was at a loss, her face so belied
her words. Then taking up a glass of wine, I did
as I had seen others do already — held it towards
her, bowed, smiled, and said: "Proceed, mistress,
I am listening," and drank part of the wine.

"Good!" said she. "Well, then, I learned from
my father to-night that a famous — famous — agent
of Sir Henry's was found gagged and bound in the
top of a half burned house at the foot of Broadway
last night — your face, man, your face!" she laughed,
suddenly.

"Tell us of the joke, Mistress Philipse!" called
Captain Atherton across the table.

"Ah, 'tis a secret, Captain," said she, brightly,
"between Mr. Merton and myself. We are plotting

the ruin of some one." Then turning to me, still
with a smile on her lips, but a strange pleading in
her eyes, "I do not know what is being done. But
he is a secret agent whom no one knows, so that it
must be kept quiet. But — but — they are searching with all the forces and power at their command
to find the man who did it. All that noise outside
last night was the attack being made to capture him.
They may — they may find him!"

"And if they do?"

"They will kill him without trial, or the knowledge
of any one but themselves!"

I knew it well, and had all day. Yet 't is not in
me to deny that a cold shiver ran up my spine, as
I stood up with the others and drank at the baron's
call the health of "their Gracious Majesties the King
and Queen," and I took what there was in my glass.

"I am sorry for the man, whoever he be."

"God guard him!" whispered the girl under her
breath with a white face.

"Pinch your cheeks, mistress," said I, smiling,
"for I think the captain fears the joke is but a poor
one."

Her face lit with a quick, natural smile.

"'T was not you, then, was it? Tell me!"

"Rather tell Major Sproat on your right the pith
of the joke," said I, and I took to myself the rest
of the glass of burgundy, for the wine was good for
the nerves, and before we were done there were five
kinds set before us.

In a moment or two she turned again to me.

"That was a capital story," I said. "Tell me the other you mentioned. — Ah! 't will be less amusing I can see from your sorrowful face!" But the girl that I had seen stand up before five ruffians in the foul tavern was as game here as there. She changed the expression of her face, but she could not alter the look in her eyes. For a moment she crumbled a bit of bread at her plate, looking at it, and then:

"There is not much of a story, and what there is of it is but an old and common tale."

"Yet I would hear it, if I may," I answered.

"There was once a young girl — a foolish wench — who was bidden by her parent to a good marriage."

"Ah!" said I. "'T is a fairy tale. And why was the wench a foolish wench?"

"A fairy tale, indeed," she answered, "but this foolish wench would none of this good marriage, because the man was a mean and cowardly wretch, and — and — " she had turned to me a little, her hand still crumbling the bread, one white arm resting on the cloth, the other hand in her lap, quivering on her silken dress, and her fair white bosom rose and fell quickly, as if it would burst her bodice, but finding that too strong would escape above it; " — and she was forced to do this thing, this dreadful thing, by her father's wish — "

"And," said I, suddenly, "she ran away to escape it? — "

"And was brought back to it," she added, giving me a long look that stirred the very soul in me, "was brought back to it, because the good man of

the good marriage held the fortunes of her father
in the palm of his hand — "

"Thy face is a beautiful but an open book, Mistress Deborah," said I, interrupting her, "and there
be those here that can read, I fear. — So! That
closes the volume partly," for she had straightened
up a bit, and a little pitiful smile struggled at the
corners of her mouth. God knows I could have
taken her in my arms there before them all, had
I dared, and comforted her in her loneliness and
trouble, and bade her have no fear. But I only
said between my teeth:

"What did this good man to her?"

"He threatened her always, and tried to force her
to it, and held up the ruin of her family — he has,
indeed, time and again!"

"Curse the coward!" said I, softly.

"And — and she had no one to help her — in
this fairy tale — until she saw some one — "

"Aye, dear heart, he is found," said I. "What
shall he do?"

"If he would meet her and let her — "

"Where and when?"

"To-morrow night beyond the Vauxhall Gardens
a few rods, by a clump of four great trees."

"He will be there! And stay — let the princess
in the fairy tale have the good man meet her there,
too! — Aye, do as I bid, girl!" I added, as a frightened
look came into her eyes.

"You are a good friend, Merton — Mr. Merton,"
said she, softly, as her head bent for a moment,

And there under the table, my foot touching hers, I put mine upon it and gave the only pressure of sympathy vouchsafed to me. Up over her face to her white forehead and on into her hair went a sweet flush that seemed to draw a smile after it, playing about her lips and into her beautiful eyes.

Strange that just then I caught a warning look in the baroness' face as she talked on to the Prince. But I did see it, and, not knowing what to do, drank off again at a gulp another glass of wine.

The little shoe fluttered under my boot, but did not withdraw, and for a moment we sat there quiet in the midst of that bustling, laughing, gossiping room full, with glasses clinking and toasts tripping up and down the board. And as the hostess rose and all followed her example I caught a strange look in young Atherton's eyes — where the fiend had I seen that face before? — that at this moment was enough to set me on fire as I stepped back to hand my supper partner to the door of the drawing-room. There I gave her to the fair young baroness, and saw them lock arms affectionately and walk on into the other room close together, but saying not a word.

"Draw up to this end of the table, gentlemen," cried the host, cheerfully. "Let us give the health of His Royal Highness!" And so we stood and drank again, and in good truth, what with my strange conversation and the two great pieces of news I had heard within an hour, I found I had had enough for one man, more than enough for one who had not been blessed with a hard head that paid

14

little heed to the fumes of wine. 'T was evident that some of the others had fared worse and drunk more. Tryon, who took the chair next the Prince as we sat down on either side of him, let out the buttons of his waistcoat, and sat back puffing out his cheeks between his words, as if the purple veins had more than they could well carry.

"Baron," puffed he in a gruff voice, "where got ye this fine old burgundy? 'T is a rare bottle, as I 'm damned! Have ye not found it to your Highness's taste?" turning to the young prince.

"Indeed I have," said the latter. "There 's none better in London, I 'll be sworn."

"'T is but just come in the last packet," replied the baron. "And Sir Henry would not hear but I should take some of it."

"'T is helped by the voyage, indeed it is," puffed the governor again. "What 's this we hear of the rebel Washington's silly trick with Rochambeau?"

"Mr. Merton could tell us much if he would," answered Major Purdy. I was in the act of lighting my clay pipe when this startling answer froze me as I sat with the taper in my hand; and then I took a long breath as he went on, "He 's just come from Newport. Is it not so, sir?"

"Oh, aye!" cried the governor. "You are the messenger that saw Sir Henry last night, eh?"

"The French are safe and sound in Newport," said I. "And like to stay there."

"Let 'em be safe in hell, as soon as they will," said the general, "and all the rest of the frog-eating traitors."

"A health to the governor!" cried Major Sproat, getting heavily to his feet. "And damnation and confusion to the rebels all! May the whole lot rot in prison soon!" Down went more wine, and whether 't was the drink in me or the thought of to-morrow night, I was near up at him for his cursed British toast. I moved my chair to join some of the younger men, and found myself close to Atherton, who was droning a song through his tipsy lips.

"Aye!" said he, "good! 'T is a proper sentiment. To hell with them all! But I 'll give ye another. I 'll bid ye drink to the brightest pair of eyes in the town, that were but just now not a hundred yards from our friend here."

"Good! Good!" cried Prince Henry, and they drank what I and all knew to be a toast to Mistress Philipse.

"They say her cousin Pendleton's case goes by hard roads," said a young fellow in a big red coat, "and that she 'll none of him in spite of her father."

"I would I had his chance," mumbled Atherton. "I 'd win by fair or foul means, and that soon, too! For there 's no finer bit of female flesh in the colonies."

I cursed the drunken beast under my breath, and held to my chair to keep myself from driving his words down his throat.

"He 'll win her yet," said Sproat. "They tell me Sir Henry is none too sure of the father's loyalty, and some of the family, so 't is whispered, are starving with the rebels at this moment." At this I pricked up my ears, and the strange fleeting resemblance she bore to Rob Curtis came to my mind.

"I heard to-day, too," laughed a young subaltern, "that a reconnoissance was foiled at the Judge's country house up above Gowan's Ferry but a week ago, and some good fellows lost. 'T is rumoured the old man knew somewhat of how 't was done."

The sweat came out in beads on my forehead. Had I perhaps made her lot the harder by my work? Curse these scandal-mongers for fools!

"Tut! tut!" laughed Atherton, leaning forward and leering at the company. "There's more behind that little episode than Sir Henry knows."

"What is it, man?" cried one or two drawing towards him.

"The little girls will have their fling, eh, your Highness? And she is no saint, they say, and a reconnoissance may not always be to study the enemy."

The crew laughed out, and cried to know the story.

"Nay, boys, you should not hear it. 'T will take your thoughts from the cause," said Atherton, leaning back and looking over the company with a patronising air.

But they cried out for it, and, with my breath coming quick and short, I leaned forward too.

He slowly drank another glass and looked about him. Then, lowering his voice, he said:

"The house is in neutral country, and empty, and the lady has been on a little visit — a little visit, you understand — somewhere, and a well-known coach was found hard by broken down. I saw it myself, for

I was up there on special duty. And my little wench
could spend a day or two in peace and quiet with her
cavalier — "

" 'T is a foul lie! " I cried, striking the table with
my fist till the glasses jumped about, and rising, I
stood over him, scarce realising what I had done. For
I knew him now well. 'T was the " jolly good fellow "
of Gowan's Tavern!

They were all on their feet in an instant, excepting
Atherton, who looked at me with a cool smile on his
face.

" And what pup are you, my colonial squire, that
trot about telling gentlemen they lie? "

" Do not burden your dull brain to learn who I
am. 'T is but a cowardly gentleman, as you call yourself, who would blacken the fair name of a woman
over his cups. Therefore I tell ye, ye lie! The girl
is as pure as snow! "

Slowly he got upon his feet as the whole company
stood dumbfounded for a moment, and with a savage
look in his eye made a step towards me and lightly
slapped me on the cheek before I could move. I had
him by the throat in an instant, and would have choked
the wind out of him, had not the whole company
jumped between us and pulled us apart.

" Let me alone! " cried he, with a white face, as half
a dozen held him by the arms.

" Silence! " roared the governor. " What in hell's
name do ye mean here in the presence of your superior officers! Patterson," cried he, turning to the
commandant, " you 'd better commit 'em both. Why,

damme, do you think you're in a tavern with a lot of low pimps? Have ye no respect for a Prince of the Blood? And you, sir, whoever ye be," continued he, getting more red and furious at each word as he turned to me, "do ye think ye can bring your clownish colonial manners here and tell people they lie?"

"'T was a foul lie against a fair name," said I, looking him in the eye.

"Why, God — a — mercy!" yelled the old fellow, fairly jumping up and down. "The man tells me I lie, too!"

But General Patterson and the baron stepped forward, the one coming up to me, the other taking the governor by the arm.

"Mr. Merton," said the commandant, slowly but coolly to me, "and you, Captain, shake hands!"

We both hesitated.

"Shake hands this moment and sit down, or you will be in irons in ten minutes! — Well, will ye, or not?" he continued, his voice rising and a dark look coming into his face. And then Atherton broke from his friends, laughing a forced laugh, and held out his hand. I could do naught but accept it, though my heart was bitter at the action.

"Now, offer your apologies to Baron Riedesel!" commanded the general. And we did so, and sat down, glum as dormice. But Prince Henry saved the day, and I thanked him inwardly for his high sense of honour as well as his tact, for he stood up and said, as the others were silent:

"Governor Tryon, I ask you and the others to drink the health of Mistress Deborah Philipse."

"Well said, your Highness!" cried old Tryon, and we drank. But the party was killed for that night, and as we rose to go into the drawing-room Atherton came by me and said slowly:

"Do you carry a little steel tool, my young merchant?"

I nodded.

"And can ye play with it at times?"

"I can try."

"Capital!" said he, laughing. "When shall we play together?"

"The sooner the better," said I.

"Tut! tut! So hot?" said he jocosely. "'T is after midnight now. Shall we say at six in the morning, and waive formalities?"

"Where?"

"Up in the fields by Corlear's Hook. Have ye a friend in the town?"

"I have, and we will be ready at six."

He laughed again and walked jauntily off, saying:

"So, man, you carry it well for a civilian. Go now and say your prayers!"

CHAPTER XIX

HOW ONE MAY MAKE FRIENDS WITH THE ENEMY

WHEN I got back to Mrs. Hodges' I found our room empty. It was then near upon one o'clock at night, and what might have taken Acton forth I did not know. And so I sat me down to wait his coming.

My thoughts were none of the brightest, and our case was hourly becoming more serious. And yet the thought of that touch of a small slipper was more than enough to overbalance the danger of our situation and the chance of the wrecking of everything in the perhaps foolish duel I had brought on my own shoulders.

So they had set a marriage for her, — her father, and, I'd be sworn, the old aristocratic witch, too, if truth were known! The thought of it made me get up and walk around the room. Indeed, I had not known it till then, till I heard of this danger to her, but 't was true! I could not live my life without her. I could not see a future without that face by me, belonging to me, to protect and comfort and serve as I would my own life — aye, far more! Would she have told me of her trouble, would she have trusted me with it and asked my help, if she had not cared?

Could she, I tried to think, could she ask a man to save her if she did not think of him more than of others?

It could not be! In spite of her knowledge of my duty to my country, in spite of the fact that she belonged to the other side, in spite of all the impossible difficulties, she trusted me, believed in me. Could she love me? Aye, was it not fair to suppose so? I got up again and shook the chair as if it had been the hand of a friend. She could not! She could not! God would not deceive a man so! And if that were true, then let come what would! I was young and strong, and I would win her to myself. I would! I would! A man cannot be asked to write down the dark thoughts that will crop up into his brain — I could think of none but her! Let the cause be what it would, she should be mine though the soulless rocks and hills of the land were ruled by king or president! Could I not live in joy and happiness all the days of my life even in the depths of hell, if she were by my side? And what could it be to me whether the edicts came from this side of the water or the other? Nothing! Nothing! She was my love, and I cared little of what might become of aught else! What did I care for Arnold? He was a wretched traitor to his country. Let him live or die, I cared not a whit! What was the fiend Hazeltine? Nothing to me. Let him do his worst, live or die! I had not known it — I had not guessed it in myself till this night. I loved her! I loved her because she was beautiful, because of her high and fearless look that told of a fearless heart. She would do what she would; let no man guess otherwise. I loved her because of her own dear self as she sat in that little gown with her arms and throat shaming the whiteness of the cloth beneath the glasses, and with God's good help she should know it soon! — and Acton came in and sat down and looked at me.

"How long have you been here, friend?" asked he.

"But a moment."

"Has aught happened? Any one come?"

"No."

"Then there will be one here soon. They 're hunting us close," said he, coolly.

"I care not a tinker's dam."

"What ails thee, man?" asked he, leaning forward in his chair and looking at me closely.

"Nothing."

"Well, let 's to bed. There 's much to do to-morrow. We must take the boards from Arnold's fence by the water to-morrow evening."

"I do not know that we can."

He turned quickly on me, looking at me with his great honest blue eyes, and then, walking up to me, he put his two big hands on my shoulders, towering over me, and said again:

"What ails thee, man?"

"Nothing."

"Merton," said he, in his boyish way, "do ye forget, man, that there 's hundreds, perhaps thousands of our men's lives depending on the capture of this Hazeltine?"

"I do not much care."

He stood looking at me in wonder for a moment, and then, gripping me with his strong hands, he said:

"I do not know thee, Merton! What would Rob Curtis say to thy mood? Hast forgotten thy honour and let it sleep? Wake up, friend, and remember the trust the great Washington has put in you! I do not know all you have to do. You have not told me. But what's to be done must be done quickly, or you and I and Curtis will be dead and nothing done."

"I am a crazy fool," I muttered.

"That ye are not, Merton," said he with a kindly smile. "But something has happened, and you shall tell me."

And he sat me down and drew out of me the lie I gave Atherton over the wine, and the sequel that was coming in the morning at six. At that he laughed a free laugh, and cried:

"Why, man, I've seen ye in worse places than that and never knew you to take on so. Is he so marvellous a sword?"

I could not tell him the truth, and thought best to let him think so, and he thereupon began to talk to me in an embarrassed fashion, telling me I had too good a hand to lose in such a child's play, and more and more, till I must needs smile at his ill-concealed desire to bring me out of my supposed dread or fear to meet this man. And so we talked softly together through the night as men talk but seldom in a lifetime, as no one could write down on paper, of home and friendship and chivalry to one's God and one's commander. And I learned in those few hours something of the soul of a great honest man, awkward when he got upon such subjects, but with as high a view of life and honour and the love of good women as it has pleased God to let me hear from the lips of any one, or see in the eyes of any human being, save only one, and that, Heaven be thanked, no man! And in those few hours cropped up a friendship of man to man between us two that through many a trial has lasted on to this day, and will till the death of us both, and after.

And so it came to five in the morning, a sultry autumn morning, still dark when we went down Beaver Street and through Princess to Queen Street, and thence down Cherry Street to the shipyards by the breastworks at Rutgers, and to the hill and fields at Corlear's Hook. We had not gauged the distance well and were a bit late in arriving, so that it was striking six in the barracks hard by when we came into the fields above the tide that flows between Long Island and Manhattan. The place was rolling country dotted with trees and undergrowth, and I had begun to think we should not find the others when I heard a hail and saw the party in a small hollow below us and nearer the river. There was a soft mist hanging in the bottom like that of an August morning, and we could make out half a dozen figures looming up as we came down to them.

"Here they are at last," said a voice that made me start, for I recognised it as that of Dr. Low, the chirurgeon, who had laid out with me not twenty-four hours before the plan of abducting Arnold. Then stepped up Prince Henry, Major Sproat, and Lieu-tenant Purdy, and last came Captain Atherton.

"We have come to see fair play done, sir," said the young Prince. "And to be in sufficient force to pre-vent any interruption from the authorities, should such occur. You know all here but Dr. Low, I think."

"What name was it?" asked the doctor, shaking hands in a business-like way, as if he saw me for the first time.

"Mr. Merton and Mr. Roberts," said Major Sproat, presenting us.

"Well, gentlemen, if you insist on this, 't is time 't was over," said Low, and the major and Acton then measured my sword and Atherton's. Finding them practically the same length, they led us to the bottom of a hollow and into an open bit surrounded by trees, and just as the light was fairly full grown for another day we were ready.

Acton was in his element. He talked in an offhand way with the others, hoped Atherton was a good hand, as his friend there was no fool, and asked:

"What's the rules?"

"The first serious draw of blood settles the affair, Dr. Low deciding," said the Prince, "if you will agree."

"My friend is quite at your disposal, gentlemen," said Acton, bowing, while I walked up and down by myself. I had had so little time to think on the affair that the serious nature of it had not occurred to me, and now for the first time I began to think of what might happen to myself. If a stroke found me home and did for me, I did not much care. But I had a horror of a serious wound so that I should live on here and fail in my work. My death was nothing to any one but General Washington, and he alone would know of my falling away from his commands.

"Well, gentlemen, is all ready?" said the doctor.

We stepped out and drew. The two blades crossed, holding there for a moment as each of us took a good look at the other. I was to do as I had done many times before in open fights upon a skirmish — wait to feel the strength of his wrist. He tried to do the same, but becoming irritated he made three quick passes at me, and, though his blade did not leave mine once, I knew I had a strong hand that had been in a long and a good school.

Just as the third thrust came and I parried, I swung my point down, turned it under his blade, and swayed his point out to the left of me. It would have been my first thrust *en quatre*, had not a voice cried out:

"Stop where you are, gentlemen, in the king's name!"

We both stopped, turned, and saw three men coming down the slope above us. They were in our midst in a moment.

"Gentlemen, I come with the warrant for the arrest of that man," and I took a sudden breath as I saw Hazeltine standing there pointing at me, "and this man here," pointing to Acton. Acton laughed in his face.

"What is this, sir?" cried Prince Henry, walking over to Hazeltine. "Do you not see you interrupt an important matter?"

"Your Highness, I am obliged to follow the orders of Sir Henry. These men are being searched for all over this town. It is a matter of great military importance."

"And can you not choose a better time, then?" asked the young man in the first tone of voice I had heard him use that showed me he was accustomed to issue rather than receive orders.

"I cannot do it, your Highness," said Hazeltine, doggedly, and none too politely.

"Frank," cried Atherton at this, "'t is an ill-selected moment. What matters half an hour?"

"It matters much," said the other hotly. "They must come now!"

"Must?" said Sproat, in a questioning tone.

"Certainly, major."

"Then, my friend," said the Prince, quietly, "listen to me. The military demands have nothing to do with this. We will go on with our affair. Therefore leave us alone and arrest your men later as you can." And he started to turn on his heel.

"I shall be obliged to use force," cried Hazeltine. The young Prince turned about as if the speaker had touched a spring in his mechanism. But before he could speak Dr. Low said softly:

"If you attempt anything of the sort you will simply become our prisoners! These two gentlemen have come here relying on our honour. They no sooner arrive than they are arrested. May it not appear to them that this is an ambush?"

"In fact, some such thing might stray into our brains," said Acton blandly.

"Therefore," said the Prince, "our own honour is here at stake, and we will, with your permission, or in fact without it, continue our affair and deliver these gentlemen where they came from in safety, or my name is not Guelph."

Hazeltine glared around him for a moment and put his hand on a pistol, but the movement started the others, and before he could draw, six men surrounded his three and stood ready for anything.

"'Tis a piece of treachery to your Highness's august father," cried the man.

"I'll look out for that," said the Prince haughtily.

"You know not what you do! It will cost you your commissions, gentlemen, and, by God, I'll do my duty!" And he turned to his men and pointed at me.

Atherton stepped in front of me, as did the doctor, and for an instant we all thought a short but serious affair was beginning. Sproat put his hand on Hazeltine's shoulder as if to say something. But the other threw it off fiercely, and the dark hatred the man bore me showed in his face as he turned to me and cried:

"Have another half hour, you fool! I'll see you hanged before night, mark me there!" and he started to move off.

"Stay, man," said the doctor. "You must remain till this is over. And you two men," continued he, "stand there before Major Sproat and Lieutenant Purdy, and do you, sir, remain by me. Now, gentlemen, I think we can begin again."

I had less taste for it than ever, after the quick action of Atherton when he thought I was to be attacked. But we were soon at it, and as I got into the work and my head cooled down, the thought of her against whom this man's jest had been directed stiffened my wrist and set me hard at him.

He played his rapier well after the orthodox fashion of duelling, and twice touched me, but not through the skin. Then, seeing that I stood on the defensive still, he began to grow red in the face and his eyes lit up with anger. Not a sound came from the others as we circled around one another, nor did I say a word until he began to press me hard, forward and back, forward and back, each time a different stroke. Then I exclaimed in surprise unconsciously, for he seemed to be a new man. My breath came hard and fast, and I began to take the offensive. Twice, thrice, four times he parried, and then on a sudden on he came and I felt a sting in my left arm just at the biceps.

Dr. Low called a halt, and ripped up my sleeve in spite of my cries that 't was nothing.

"Leave me alone," cried I. "Do you not see 't is but a scrape? Come, sir, do not waste your time!" And I broke away and made at him with my temper half gone. We went it hot after that, nor do I remember anywhere such quick work. Once I was down on my knees. Twice he saved his life by a prodigious side jump. And then — then I saw him come

15

at me from below, his point up and falling as he rose himself.

'T was a stroke, a gasp, for I could do naught but strike his point down and then put all my strength of arm, wrist, and body to turn my blade under his. I did so, God knows how, but in an instant I felt my point at his hilt and with a wrench his rapier jumped twenty feet away. By the force of the twist he was swung half round sideways to me, and, tripping over his own feet, he fell towards me — 't was all so quick I could not tell how 't happened — but I suddenly felt my sword touch his left side under the arm, and instinctively I jumped back and drew my blade away. Down he went, flat on his side, with one foot twirled around the other, and I stood waiting as he got up.

The others jumped forward to him. But he pushed them hastily aside and strode up to me, as I stood there dazed and panting, and grasped my hand. Not a word did he say for an instant. Then, turning to the others:

" My friends, 't is a new thing for Atherton to do. But you saw him! He could have run me through by standing still, and I say, by God, I 'll fight no more with such a man! " Then, turning to me, he went on: " Mr. Merton I was drunk last night, and what I said — "

" Not another word, Captain," said I. " 'T is over, and, thank God, no harm done. Let the thing die here and now."

They crowded about me and shook my hand, and

said I know not what that I had done, and quite
naturally the Prince said:

"And now to Fraunce's Tavern for breakfast."
And, moving off, we left Hazeltine and his two men
on the field without a word. But after passing the
shipyards they went on into Rutgers Street, and just
before we came to Cow Foot Hill the whole party,
Acton and I with them, turned suddenly into a garden
and entered what I found later was the famous Walton
Mansion of the Rutgers family, where the Prince for
the time lived.

'T was a magnificent mansion with great pieces of
furniture; the banquet hall alone as large as two
ordinary dwellings. We passed into the hall and
through it into a library, where sat a table covered
with bottles and cold food, enough for a hundred, it
seemed to me. I could not but express my surprise
at this plenty and magnificence in the midst of so
much poverty and scarcity elsewhere in the city.

"Ah, you do not know how we live," cried Sproat.
"For whole weeks we eat nothing but salt beef, and
then in comes a foraging party, and the whole town
gorges for a week."

The young Prince took the head of the table and all
set to work in the hot, murky air, opening bottles and
dishing out the food. No one waited on us, and we
were indeed a jovial party, all there but the doctor,
who said he must go, and looked at me meaningly as
he added:

"Come to my office, young man, when you've
eaten, and let me dress your arm." Indeed, what

could be a simpler way of completing my plan with
him than by this ordinary appointment. Strange that
I should be sitting with these enemies of my country
and yet growing to like them! Strange that I should
be deceiving men that, whatever else they might be,
were men of honour through and through! Strang-
est of all, that Atherton could not do enough for me
since my unconscious saving of his life!

No one referred to my near arrest, nor questioned
us as to its cause. And Acton soon had them roar-
ing with laughter with his quaint remarks and his
jovial songs. The only thing I noticed was a man at
the rear door and another at the front in the hall, both
standing motionless and evidently watching to guard
that we should not be surprised.

"Mr. Merton," cried the Prince, rising, "you are
a good sword and a better gentleman, and I give ye
long life and the girl most to your heart!"

"Nay, nay, sir," cried I, for the wine went to the
proper spot, and I felt at least one load off my back
since the early morning, "'t is the wrong order. A
toast to His Royal Highness first!"

There was a cry of applause. But he would not
have it so. And, I still insisting, we stood there,
glasses in hand, laughing and protesting and all talking at once, till Acton in his big voice roared that
't was a shame to lose the chance to drink the wine,
and Atherton cried out:

"So it is! Then I give you them both! The first
gentleman of Europe and the first gentleman of the
last hour!"

Out must come another roar of applause, and so
went the toast. And as the major dipped out the
newly-made punch from a huge bowl, Acton set the
key for "Landlord, fill the flowing bowl," and we
roared out the song into one another's ears, standing,
and with the glasses in our hands, turning now to
one, now to another, with the glasses clinking, some
beating time with the left hand, till Atherton began
a marching movement around the table, and we all
must needs fall into line, tramping round and round,
and yelling out the brave old song over and over
again. Finally we flopped down into chairs, and up
jumped Sproat and cried:

"An' now, gentl'm'n," and he held up his glass,
"now, confus'n t' our en'mies! Egad! I'm a bit
confus'd mesel, ho! ho! 'S a joke! D'ye see? 'S
a joke, 's I'm a sinner! Ho! ho! ha! ha!"

"Confus' 'em, if ye like," roared Acton, "but they're
brave men, too!"

"Aye, so the' are! S'th' are!" cried the Prince,
banging his hand down on the table with a thump
and a swish that sent half of the bottles crashing on
the floor. "I've learned that since I've been here.
And we Britishers always want a good en'my. Eh,
my friends, is 't not so, eh?"

"S''t is! So 't is, y'ighness!" roared the crowd.

"Confusion and good luck to 'em!" cried Atherton.

"Aye, good luck to 'em!" I cried, putting my glass
high above my head. In a moment Atherton was on
the table, and we standing round him on the floor trying to reach our glasses up to his.

"Good luck to 'em," cried the crowd, and down went the extraordinary toast with no heel-taps for at least two in that jovial gang.

As they began another song — those that could sing more — the young Prince came round to me and said unsteadily:

"Now's your time, Merton. Out by the garden, and good luck to ye. I don't know your trouble, but you've got no harm at our hands," and he held out his own. I thanked him and got Acton away and out into Cherry Street in the warm sun, and so on by Queen Street to our boarding-house. There I left him singing snatches to himself, and, bidding him watch out for himself and for Curtis, if he should come, I made my way to Dr. Low's.

CHAPTER XX

THE MEETING BY THE VAUXHALL GARDENS

THE shrewd chirurgeon no sooner saw me than he took me into a little back room, and there we sat most of the afternoon, laying out the plan for Arnold's abduction. The house at No. 3, which the traitor occupied, had a garden that ran down to the waters of the Hudson and was surrounded by a high board fence. Low had the whole plan, though he could not take active part, as he must be ready in the future for many such affairs, and had thus to keep himself above all chance of suspicion. It was a wonder to me how he had done it so long, and I told him so, saying also that I marvelled how I had escaped arrest.

"'T is simple enough," said he. "I do but attend to my work as a physician. So I enter all houses, even Clinton's, at all times, and I hear more than any one has the least hint of. What I do for the cause is done here, and always a visitor has some such reason as you have now for coming. If he is arrested, and several have been," he continued with a serious face, "I am free, and never yet has man or woman betrayed me by the slightest sign. Your case is not so sure, and I have to tell you that your episode with that man in the

old burnt house was a bad blunder. He is furious at
you for that, or something else, and were it not that
his work for Clinton is so secret that few in this city
know of it at all — and I only because I was once
treating Clinton when he arrived and the news of his
work was out before they realised it — you would be
in prison long ago. They must keep the whole thing
quiet, and no doubt they are trying to find your reason
for being here. Have more care therefore for the rest
of this day and night " — I thought of my appointment for nine — " and do not go out. I cannot help
you, if you are taken. You will simply disappear. No
public arrest, no execution, no trial for you, man!
That was why no force was sent to arrest you this
morning. Now for the plan."

The plan was simple enough. An opening had already been made in the high board fence by the water.
The boards could be taken out at a moment's notice.
We, Acton, Curtis, and I, were to approach the garden
in a boat with some trusty oarsmen, proceed through
the hole in the fence, thence through a window into
the rear of the house, opened for us by an American
soldier, who had got himself employed by Arnold on
the ground of desertion from our lines. Arnold himself was to be taken out of his bed, gagged, put into a
huge bag and carried out to the boat. Thence to
Paulus' Hook across the river, and into our lines.

'T was a simple plan and one that would have
worked as it has worked before, but for fatality, that
has more to do with making history than thousands of
great minds.

And so at dusk I left Low with a long shake of
the hand and walked slowly and carefully through the
little streets so muddy and narrow, so foul with the
smell of the burnt houses and soaked refuse that it
sickened one in those strangely hot and heavy days.
Low lived hard by the corner of Princess and Broad
Streets, and directly opposite the waste of ruins that
no hand had touched since three years before. There
in the hovels, for they were nothing better, burrowed
out of half-ruined houses, lived the scum of the great
town — the poor wretches who scarcely live, the har-
lots of the city — and there were thousands of them,
as there are in the rear of any great camp — who
beset you as you strode along the narrow, crooked,
filthy streets.

Thence I came to Mrs. Hodges', and found Acton
just returned again from the neighbourhood of No. 2
Broadway, where he had been anxiously watching for
Curtis. I told him that I fancied I had a chance of
catching Hazeltine from something I had heard by
going up to the top of the town — the more shame to
me again that I looked into his blue eyes and told him
the story — but I cannot help it, nor could I then!
'T was an affair of my own and another, and I could
not share it with him. So that he agreed to wait for
Curtis till ten o'clock, bringing him on with him; but
if he did not come then, to follow me himself to Vauxhall Gardens, for I told him the place. I, in turn, was
to get back as soon as possible to his place in an angle
of two houses where we watched for our anxiously
expected friend.

I set out and wandered along Broadway to Vesey Street, and thence down that muddy and unkempt thoroughfare among the burnt houses up Barclay Street to the college, now a prison, and thence by Chambers Street to Vauxhall Gardens. There I stopped and looked about. It must be near nine, and she had selected as deserted a spot as could be well found around the city. Beyond the gardens all was wilderness and trees and muddy roads, and a nasty mist hung over everything, that made my clothes limp and wet.

Not a soul appeared to be anywhere in sight or hearing, and so I walked slowly on by the side of the road looking for the four trees, fearing every minute lest I miss them. Suddenly I heard a clock somewhere ring out nine, and just ahead a figure stepped out into the road. I dropped into the underbrush and looked long at it, but could not make the mistake of forgetting that quick nervous movement of head and limbs I had grown to know so well.

It was she fast enough, and my heart beat a tattoo to think I was so near her in such a spot, and that she had such faith in me as this. Her sorrow must indeed be a terrible one. As I stepped out into the road she made a quick movement to disappear and then came towards me slowly.

"You have come," said she, under her breath. "This way." And soon we were off the road a hundred yards and under the gloom of four great trees standing close together. "I know not what I am doing," said she, nervously, "if you should be found here, 't would be your ruin."

"Would you grieve for that?" I asked.

"Would a wife grieve for her husband?" asked she gently.

I took her hand.

"Would you grieve sorely, sorely for me, Deborah?" I whispered.

"Tut, tut, sir," said she in the same tone, drawing her hand away. "We are not come to a tryst here."

"Ah! but now that we are here, will you not let me tell you somewhat of that which has been in my mind all day, since the dinner, aye! since many a day now?" And I took her hand again.

"That I will not, sir, nor will I permit you to press the nails out of my fingers, — if you will be so kind as to let my hand keep its shape." And yet she did not seem so angry.

"Its shape! Why, God bless it, I would no more — "

"Oh," cried she softly, and tried to draw it away, "oh, God bless it, you say, and still it is by now but a shapeless pulp, I 'll be sworn."

I lifted it to my lips once, twice, three times and then 't was gone under her black cape where I dared not follow.

"No, no, Merton," she hurried on. "This is no time for such things. You said you would help me, and he will soon be here."

"Will he come?" I asked.

"Never fear," she answered with a strange, sad smile.

"Then tell me quickly."

"I do not know how. My father is not over zealous

for the king's cause. Yet he is not disloyal to Sir
Henry in any way. But I have a dear brother some-
where on the other side and we are all suspected, and
Pendleton, my own cousin, is very powerful with Sir
Henry. And — and do you not see, you stupid?"

"And he tells Clinton your father is a traitor if
you do not smile on him, and that he is a staunch
follower of George the — of the king, if you listen to
his suit?"

"Ah! that is but the half, the little half!" said she,
her eyes glistening in the growing moonlight. "Do
you not see he holds it over me day by day and will
not let me rest? And there is something he has to tell
of papa —"

"The blackmailer!" I muttered.

"What, I know not, but I fear day and night — I
fear always — and papa must fear, too, and he does
not understand why I cannot save us all by doing this
dreadful thing, and Aunt Mary —"

"What, the old — er, that is — Madam De Lancy?"

"Yes, yes, she is nearly beside herself, for she thinks
it a good match according to her ideas. In fact," she
added with the quaint suspicion of a smile, "in fact,
she does not think it wise to marry out of the family.
No other equals it, you see."

"And he comes now —"

"To settle the matter, he thinks," she muttered,
catching at her throat.

"Aye, we'll settle the matter —"

"Oh, what will you do? I fear for this. I do not
know why I should have done it!"

"Why, dear, he cannot win you. You are married already!"

She looked up at me quickly with a smile and put her hand in mine.

"I know! I know!" she cried, softly. "But it will count for naught, and will now only make him furious and spur him on to ruin us all."

I took the hand in both mine and we stood an instant, when both started to hear the sound of some one coming through the underbrush.

"He is here," I whispered. "Now, brave heart, go out and meet him, and let me look at him and hear what he says."

She shuddered a moment and then, lifting her head as I had seen her do so often now, walked out into the moonlight. The dark figure of a man approached her quickly:

"Debby, my darling, I am here!"

Good God, that voice!

I fell back against the tree an instant, and then the woods faded away, and with them went Deborah Philipse, her father, and her crotchety old aunt, and I sprang out of the shadow and rushed straight at his chest and bore him with a heavy concussion to the ground. In an instant I had him by the throat and turned him over and got his arms up by the shoulder blades before he knew what had struck him.

"You cursed spy!" I cried. "I have you now! Do but move, and your work is over!"

'T was but the work of a moment to take the strap of my sword belt and bind his wrists together. And by taking a turn around his neck his hands were securely bound between his shoulder blades. Then I turned to her and saw her standing by in terror and bewilderment, and said what a moment later I would have given both my eyes to take back:

"Why, girl, do you know who this is?"

"He is my cousin, Frank Pendleton," she whispered with a strange doubt in her voice.

"That he may be! But he is the foulest spy in the British army, and his name is Hazeltine!"

Her change of attitude gave me a sickening sense of loss. She shrank back from me with a cry, and looked at me as if her eyes would burn into my soul.

"You! You!" she cried, hoarsely.

"I? What of me?" said I, vaguely.

"You have led me here to decoy him? You have stood here and — and — talked to me so that you might do this wretched thing?"

"I?"

"You coward!" she cried, bitterly. "And I — what a fool — what a fool I was!" and she sank down on the wet grass in a hysterical fit of tears and laughter.

But her moods flew after one another too fast to be understood. She was up in an instant.

"Come, Frank, let us go and leave this — this wretch to himself."

"But listen to me, Deborah, you do not understand —"

"Do not dare to speak to me! What can I fail to understand?"

"But this man is a spy whom I am here to —"

"Then, if you would not let what you have said to me be a great falsehood, unbind him and let him go!"

I looked at her standing before me, waiting for my reply, and groaned aloud at the misery of it. Then she turned from me with utter contempt and started towards him as he rose to his feet.

I drew my pistol, and pointing it within two feet of his breast I said:

"If you move but a step I'll fire! — Mistress Philipse, do not touch that man!"

"So it is true! it is true! Oh, you coward! You coward!" and she wrung her hands and her voice broke down completely.

So we stood, misery in my heart and gloom over all the world for me, when a figure leaped out from the underbrush, and I heard the voice of Curtis cry out:

"So you've got him! You've got him, Balfort, at last! I should know that cape and figure in a crowded —"

A piercing cry was his answer, and the next moment Mistress Philipse was lying in his arms, crying as if her heart would break. I heard an exclamation of surprise break from him as he said in sudden bewilderment:

"How came you here, Debby? What is it? Stop, and tell me the trouble."

"Oh Rob, my dear, dear brother," she cried. "Take me away from this dreadful place! Take me away! and save Frank from that man!"

I saw him make a sudden movement. He stood a

moment and then set her quickly away from him. A
stride brought him up to Hazeltine, and grasping the
man by the arm he turned him around so that they
stood face to face.

"God in Heaven!" whispered the astounded man
hoarsely, as Hazeltine stood looking him in the face
without a word. Curtis gazed at him long and steadily, as if he were coming out of a dream. Then he
twirled Hazeltine about again and looked at his back
as the man stood with his long cape over his shoulders.
A moment, and the dazed man had turned the other
face to face again.

"Great God in heaven!" he groaned under his
breath.

"Well, cousin, do you know me?" said Hazeltine
with a forced attempt at hilarity.

"Do I know thee, thou foul spy? Do I know thee?
Aye, now I do! But not till this moment did I suspect
the fiend Hazeltine could be my own cousin, Frank
Pendleton!"

"'T is a mistake, Rob. You have the wrong man."

"He lies, Curtis!" I cried, "lies in his teeth! I've
followed him and caught him now, and bound him,
and we have but to take him across the river to fill
one of the orders that sends us here."

"Never fear, Merton. I could never mistake that
figure. I've followed him these three months," and
I saw his strong face set in grim resolution and turned
to look at Mistress Philipse. She was standing by in
silent horror at what she had heard, but as she saw me
approaching her she ran to Curtis.

"My brother, will you not protect me from this man?"

"Why, Debby dear, do you not know Merton Balfort? What harm would he do you? None, dear sister, none."

"He has already! He led me here to decoy our cousin Frank to his ruin. And — I — I — " and she broke down completely again.

"'T is not so, Mistress Philipse. I came — "

"Do not dare to address a word to me, sir," cried the girl, jumping from her brother's side and stamping her foot. And she was back again sobbing in his arms.

"'T is a gross misunderstanding, Curtis," said I at my wits' ends. "You are her brother?" He nodded. "I felt it long ago! I knew it, aye, knew it all along! Yet did I never understand it till now! Well, then, I came here to help her in — in another matter — look not at me so, Robert Curtis! my conscience is as clear as a bell — but when I came here this man appeared and I knew him at once for Hazeltine, and no more suspected his relationship to you and to her than you did ten minutes ago."

"'T is a lie!" cried the girl, passionately. "A gross — "

"Mistress Philipse, I cannot answer you as I would a man. I can but say to you — aye, swear to you — that you are wrong. And may God forgive you for your hard words and your lack of faith in one who — who — would watch over your welfare!"

"I cannot understand the thing," muttered Curtis.

"Let us get this man away in safety, friend," said

16

I. "And then I will explain." And I walked up to
Hazeltine and bade him precede me.

"'T is impossible," said Curtis.

"'T is *what?*" cried I, wheeling about at him.

"He cannot go thus to the Commander-in-Chief,"
replied the man with that quiet firmness and distinct-
ness that always belonged to him. "'T will be simply
an execution by hand."

"Aye, that it will, man, and the sooner and simpler
the better," said I.

"It is quite impossible," he repeated in the same
tone.

"Robert, my friend, ye have lost your bearings.
Do you take your sister and leave him to me," and I
signed to Hazeltine to move towards the road.

"Merton, if you attempt to remove this man, you
must first cross swords with me," said Curtis in a cold
wiry voice, the more terrible in its meaning because
its tone was not raised one whit beyond the ordinary.

"What mean you, man?" asked I in amazement,
unconsciously drawing my sword an inch or two. He
did not move, but, folding his arms, said in the same
cold voice:

"Precisely what I say. If you try to remove him
you must first overcome me, and whatever the result
of our struggle, there will be more than time for him
to make good his escape." Then, turning to Hazeltine,
he walked slowly up to within a foot of him, with
folded arms, and said slowly and distinctly in that
same wiry voice:

"Frank Pendleton, you are my own cousin. Therefore shall you not, if I can prevent it, go to the gallows, as God knows you should. But I have within this hour learned that you are the veriest traitor in this land; for you have acted as spy to both armies in this war, and therefore shall you not go from this spot till either I have killed you or you me. Turn round."

"Do not do it, Curtis," I cried. "'T is a foolish sense of honour, and the man does not belong to us." But he proceeded, and soon Hazeltine's arms were free.

Curtis did not even look at me, but kept his eye on Hazeltine all the time, only vouchsafing:

"Hold thy peace, Merton! This affair is between only God, that man, and me." And they were at it there in the dim moonlight before he had finished speaking. And a weird sight it was to see these two men, one fighting to save his life, knowing he must cope afterwards with me, the other, cool, sure, as fine a swordsman as I ever saw, standing for his honour and crossing swords with his own cousin whom he had lived and played with through all their boyhood, whom now he detested, but would not hang. And under the dim blue light of the moon a few yards away stood the girl, watching them with wide eyes, silently.

I hovered about them with drawn sword, resolved that, honour or no honour, this man should not escape, but restrained more by my instinctive respect for Curtis's standards than by any sense of chivalry from taking active part. So in my bewilderment and with the misery of this episode in my heart I did not see till too late how Hazeltine, as he twisted about, gradually approached the big trees, nor guess his purpose, until on a sudden he made two long lunges and then, turning tail like any cur, darted in under them and hidden by the darkness made off. I fired both my pistols at him, but he was gone. And then I turned on Curtis:

"Now you see what your miserable honour has done for us!" I cried.

"What matter," answered he coolly. "It but shows him the greater dastard."

"But what good does that do, since your idiotic standard has let the man go? 'T will be a fine reason to give to our general! And do you perchance realise that neither your life nor mine is worth a penny from now on?"

"The coward!" said Curtis quietly, as he sheathed his sword. "Who could have thought he would so run from a fair fight? Fear not, man!" he added hastily, as I made a gesture of disgust, for by that I was beyond words. "Fear not! He is not worth a thought. When I next meet him I'll crush him like a worm."

"I cannot understand you, man," cried I, bitterly. "I cannot talk of it. Let us go, in God's name, from this place." And we did.

Mistress Philipse would not speak to me, nor look at me. And as I stepped to her side, placing her between her brother and myself, she crossed in front of him to the farther side. In all that walk back she vouchsafed not a word, neither to me nor to him, and nothing happened as we walked on in silence, except

that we came upon Acton stationed some distance below, brought there by Curtis when he had arrived in
the city and decided to follow us at once, fearing an
ambuscade.

So we came to old St. Paul's churchyard, hard by
which Judge Philipse lived, and as Acton and I walked
on in silence, I saw her cling to her new-found brother,
and heard her sob and beseech him to stay, not to
leave her. And as we passed out of earshot I could
hear her crying softly, " Oh Rob, Rob dear, why is it
all so strange and wrong, my brother dear! "

Soon he was by us again, alone, with the same cool,
calm face, that now to us, Acton and me, had a deep
and dreadful meaning in its forever sombre and sad
lines. Then we came to lower Broadway, and to No. 2,
where he bade us all enter; for, he said, we should be
found at Mrs. Hodges', and the old half-ruined house
was now free from suspicion and deserted. There we
lay for the rest of the night. I could not sleep, for my
anger at the man's escape soon faded before the
wretchedness and misery that fate and her lack of belief in me had brought upon me. I cared little whether
we were taken or not, for with this evening and day
hope and promise of the future died.

It was not true love that could doubt quickly! And,
God forgive me for it, in my hopelessness I told myself
that she was not what I had come to believe her. And
then, as I looked back upon it, I began to see that,
feeling as she did against the American cause, and
knowing what I was in the city for, she might well
think I had taken advantage of her situation to draw

my man. And I put my head in my hands, as I sat there in the darkness, and cried like any baby for the very wretchedness of it all, for the loss of so many fair hopes, for the end of a day-dream that I had thought a reality.

CHAPTER XXI

IN WHICH A WOMAN DENIES AND A MAN DIES

ALL the next day we must of necessity lie close in the old rat-hole, with one of us always on guard at a window overlooking the street. I tried to forget myself in planning for the coming night's work, and all the time another resolution was evolving in my head. We laid the whole plan before Curtis, and he approved. Once or twice he recurred to the episode of the evening before, but I could not discuss it with him. 'T was not in me to believe that his course was right, yet in the few weeks I had known him I had come to believe in him and his strong nature, and I could not but respect his code, disastrous as it had been to us.

"I cannot see the right of it, friend," said I to him. "Do not try to show it to me."

"I am sorry, Merton," he answered with a serious look. "But a man's honour is greater than his military duty."

"Let us not talk of it, man," said I again. "'T is but a failure in my duty to General Washington, and there's an end of it."

"Would you not have done the same?"

"I cannot tell, Robert. I cannot judge you, God knows! I can scarcely judge myself in this hour."

And then we recurred to the coming events.

But all the while my resolve was growing in me. The entrance to Arnold's house was set for one, at night. Then he would be sure to be at home and in bed. All the plans were arranged, and hence I would go and see her again before I left — as God lived, I would see her again! There was to be a sort of *soirée* to the Prince at the Walton House, and he had bid me come, in his offhand, friendly way. I would go.

I dared not tell my friends, for they would have held me by force, if necessary, deeming it a dangerous thing to expose myself. But this was more to me than my own life just now — aye, more than the success of our mission, though I knew they could carry that out practically as well without me, if need came.

Thus, at ten of the evening, I told them I would go to Low to see that the arrangements were completed, and despite their advice to lie close, I went out through Queen Street and so to the Walton Mansion, having first stopped at Mrs. Hodges' and got my tawdry suit. There had been a rumpus indeed. The maid, who was the only person I saw, looked at me in terror, and ran away as soon as she had let me in; and in our room there might have passed a whirlwind for the look of it.

Everything we had, which was little enough, was thrown about. The furniture was broken, and all the signs of what I rightly enough guessed must have been a military search for ourselves and whatever papers we might have had were evident. My fancy suit was picked up here and there and donned. And so I entered the Walton Mansion at the front door.

It must have been eleven of the clock, and the affair was as its height. The beautiful rooms on either side the great hall were crowded with guests, and I soon found the Prince standing to receive them. He looked at me and welcomed me with a polite bow, but a surprised look, as if to say, "Ha! my man, and so you will still be out in public!" and then I passed on, searching always but for one. My figure, my face, must have told some strange story; for people who knew nothing of me turned and looked after me and spoke together softly. But I only saw it as in a dream. On I went through the rooms, looking for but one, and not finding her.

Thus I came to the banquet hall, and to the little study beyond, where we had breakfasted the day before. And there I found her.

She was standing just inside the big hall with her back to me talking with some two or three people, her arm resting on that of a young officer whom I had not seen before. I stopped a moment, and then passing behind some large screens, set there to hide serving-tables at the corner of the room, I stood a moment to catch my wind, which seemed to strangely fail me on the moment, as if I had been running long and hard.

A moment there and I stepped out within a yard of her, still with her back to me. Again something in my face must have shown, for a lady who was talking with her, and thus facing me, looked up, and

her face changed, so that Mistress Philipse turned
to learn the cause.

She saw me. I looked at her a moment and then
stepped forward to greet her. Heaven forgive her!
On the instant she looked straight at me, straight
through me, and said in a cold, haughty voice to her
companion:

"Captain, I feel a sudden cold draught. Let us
move on."

And she turned her back on me and walked slowly
away.

I put my hand to my eyes, and stood so a moment.
Then the need of the open air came to me, and I
stepped back behind the screen and leaned far out of
an open window, trying vainly to loose the collar of
my shirt. So sitting, or rather leaning from the window, I stood, how long no one — least of all I —
could tell, neither thinking nor conscious of pain, till
I heard a strident voice back of me on the other side
of the screen saying in an evident attempt at a low
tone:

"Yes, 't is just settled. Habberton is to take his
brigade with Barnard's and board ship on Sunday.
A battery will go ahead on Saturday night, and
they should be in Huntington Harbour by Monday
evening."

"How many men, Sir Henry?"

"Five thousand all told."

"And when will the attack begin?"

"As soon as they can reach Newport Harbour.
And you will take with you a force sufficient to —"

And I heard no more, for they had moved on.

Five thousand men — Huntington Harbour — Newport! 'T was the attack finally settled on. Sunday!
't was Monday night now. Aye, Sir Henry, I had
by the greatest chance learned the one thing I should
have learned long ago, and I cleared the sill at a
bound and went out of the garden to Cherry Street,
as I had done but yesterday morning.

Walking by the lower part of the town and up
through Beaver Street, so I came to our abode and
told my friends the great news. And then I went off
to a back window and sat by myself, looking out
upon the night black with heavy clouds to add to its
blackness, but as light as day compared with my
heart and thoughts. And so they found me when it
came time for us to leave, and I went with them,
longing for something such as this desperate attempt
to cool my blood and clear my mind.

How could she do it! Might she not have had a
better faith in me? Nay, there was something wrong
with the world, if a woman who had looked into my
eyes and seen what she must have seen there could
lose her faith so wholly. How could she do it!

We came to the lane running down to the water
by Arnold's house and found our boat and boatmen
so hid beneath the bank that it was no easy matter
to find them, though we knew well they must be
there.

Curtis, as seemed always natural, took the command, and in a few moments we had loosened the
boards and were up through the garden to the house

and to the window. It stood open, and Curtis was half way in when he leaned back and stood looking at our man, who had entered the household as a military servant to do the work there for us.

"What is it, man?" asked I in a whisper.

"Gone!" said he.

"Gone?" we cried together.

"Aye! I have been searching for ye all the night, but could not find ye anywhere. Ye were not at your place in Mrs. Hodges'. Ye were nowhere in the streets. I could not find ye at all!"

"But speak up, my man," said Curtis. "What mean you?"

"He's ordered to a command on the Long Island shore and gone there."

"When?"

"Late this afternoon, just at dark."

I laughed for the very absurdity and wretchedness of it. 'T was the last straw, and our whole work and mission was gone! The others stood inactive on the news of it, and just then came one of the crew running up from the boat.

"Quick, Lieutenant," he cried, under his breath, to me. "Quick, they 're on us!" And we distinctly heard a cry down by the shore:

"There they are! Pull, men, pull!"

I was down the garden path in an instant, Acton close on to me, Curtis following leisurely. And as we came to the shore and leaped into the boat there came another large barge with half a dozen or mayhap eight men pulling towards us. Standing in the bow was a man hailing us in the voice of Hazeltine, for I call him by that name still, as so I knew him.

"Who are you here at this time o' night?"

"Frank," said Curtis, before I could speak, "Frank, take yourself and your men away, as you love your life!" And his voice rasped out the words, as if they would cut the night air.

"Oho! cousin, I have you all three," cried he. "Row on, men, hard! Into them! Into them!"

The next moment they struck us, and after a pistol shot or two that hit no one a fierce hand-to-hand fight began across the gunwales of the two boats. They were two more than we, but with the exception of Hazeltine himself the others were sailors. We were, therefore, the better swords, and there in the darkness the mix-up was complete at first and no one uttered word or cry, till down in the stern of the now locked boats came a groan, and one of our pursuers sank into his seat.

Acton was furthest aft, Curtis next and I in the bow, so that Hazeltine and I came together.

"You cur, you!" cried the man. "I have you at last!" and he made a thrust at me with such force that, parry it as I did, the defence alone was like to have knocked me overboard on the other side. I returned the thrust, and we fought there without science or attempt at skill, but as boys would fight with broomsticks, crazy with anger. So close were we together that there was no room to move and thrust, and on the instant as he parried a blow of mine I felt my point enter something soft, and, hearing a groan near by, I pulled the rapier back and saw the next man fall. Hazeltine had saved himself and killed the man next him by parrying the stroke.

At that he began to curse me for a clumsy lout, using all the foul language of which he must have been a good master, and in between his cries I could hear Acton talking to his opponents:

"So! another gone below!" cried that indomitable spirit, as he turned to the next. "Ah! one of ours!" as a fierce scream and the jarring of our boat told me one of our men was gone.

Curtis said not a word, but, his man having fallen by my chance stroke, he turned quietly to the next. None of this could I see, but I knew as if by divination without the use of eyes, for my game was near up more than once. The man fought with far more energy than he would for his cause. He hated me, and hammered at me in a frenzy, crying out that I was a coward, and a traitor, and a spy, and what not, yelling, "There! there!" each time he struck at me.

So the cries and the noise of the fight raged on close by the shore till some one falling in our boat tipped it sideways, and the two barges slipped a foot or more apart. And that foul fiend, seeing us likely to move off, gave a savage growl that I should not escape him, and, leaping on the gunwale of his boat, made a desperate thrust at me.

I saw it coming, and knew 't would reach its mark. Aye, it did so, and scraped along the ribs of my right side as if some one had gripped me with the clamps of a red-hot iron. I lost my grip on the sword and

it fell into the water just as the other boat, weighted
by Hazeltine's body on the gunwale, turned over and
tipped the whole crew, the dead, the dying, and the
living into the shallow water.

The pain I felt, the despair that was in me long
before I came to this encounter, set me doubly against
this man who had been the cause of it, and I leaped
down into the water and grappled with him there as
he stood up. No words were necessary now. We
knew that, whatever the others might do, this was
the end, and neither would let go his hold until one
of us was dead.

He was a powerful man, and though I had him by
the throat he caught me by the waist, and, putting
his foot behind me, tripped me up and we fell under
the water between the upright and empty boats — he
on top, I underneath. And there in this two-foot
depth of water we struggled and kicked and grappled
with one another for all eternity.

Lying on my back under the water, there came a
thumping in my ears and my veins began to swell.
I had no thought nor fear of death, nothing went
into my mind but a sense that I must not open my
mouth, and then, with a wrench and a struggle that I
knew must be the last, I caught him under one arm and
over his neck. 'T is an old wrestler's hold, and with
the strength of all my body and all the good years of
health and training, I bent his head down and his shoulders up till he weakened his hold on me to save his neck.

Then in an instant over he rolled under the water,
struggling, kicking, gurgling, and I — I opened my

lips and took in a prodigious gust of air, and then
closed my fingers on his throat and put one knee on
his chest, digging the other foot into the mud between his legs.

I cannot think of it even now, long years after,
without the sweat running down my spine. 'T was
frightful then. 'T is so now. For soon bubbles crept
up to the surface and burst beneath my nose, and a
horrible gurgling sound came up as if from the depths
of hell out of the water. And still I held him there,
working my frenzied fingers into his throat, till his
grip began to weaken and the bubbles came not so
fast. And still I thrust my fingers into his flesh and
held my knees hard upon his chest. And his hold
relaxed the more.

Then, of a sudden, a horror seized me of the thing
lying there beneath the water, which I could not see
but could feel warm and soft under me! I can feel
it now, and have for thirty years, and shall for as
long as I can feel anything in this body of mine — a
horror I could no more control than I could the tides
— and jumped to my feet and lifted the shapeless
mass and pitched it into the boat as she pushed her
nose into me and Curtis cried out:

"Quick, man, the guard! quick for your life!"

"And what think you, man, I care for life?" said
I, as I saw dark figures moving down the lane.

Then I gave the boat all the strength I had, and
sent her far out into the stream, calling:

"Remember, Curtis, dead or alive! dead or alive!
he goes to Washington. Remember, man! remember
as you love God, remember!"

And I was down in the shoal water crawling along the shore with nothing but my nose above the surface.

After a few yards I looked out and saw the boat far off towards Paulus' Hook and heard the crack of a dozen rifles near by fired by men who stood knee deep in the water. So I crawled on perhaps a hundred yards, and then, growing faint, and not caring much what might come of it, I crawled out on the shore and lay down in the mud and tried to breathe again. But the horror of something, I know not what, was with me and I shrivelled myself up setting my head close to my knees and holding my ankles as I lay there on one side. And I shut my eyes for fear I should see something and opened them again for fear that the unknown thing should clutch me. 'T was a terror of something horrid, unnamable, unseeable, that gripped me, and I cried out with it.

'T was but a moment when I was seized again with terror at the sound of my own voice, and a shiver ran through my bones. I lay still, looking about so far as I could without moving, for it seemed as if I must not move or stretch out a hand or foot, lest I touched that nameless something. So I lay, when all over my body broke out a sweat that burned me. I know not how long it lasted. Time was nothing then, but there in the darkness I thought long and decided to move but the least atom. It took more courage than I had ever used before to move my arm and turn over, and then, when I did attempt to do so, I could not, for something gripped and bound me in my side that drew another cry of pain and

17

terror, until I discovered it was the ugly wound his sword had made.

So I lay still — hours, it seemed — and then, reason coming to me, I got up to walk away in my drenched clothes, and staggered up through a garden to the street holding by a fence or a tree, leaning for support against the side of a house, and so into the street, just as a sign of the first light began to appear.

The gate was open and I got into the street and fell again into a heap; and then, gripping the fence, lifted myself up and stood there, as a shout came to me, it seemed from a hundred people, who rushed at me and pulled my legs from under me and picked me up. And I cared not a whit what they did nor heard a word they said, for there was not enough in life for me to trouble at it.

CHAPTER XXII

THE OLD SUGAR HOUSE

HALF conscious as I soon became, I knew only that I was being carried away, then put into a cart that jolted horribly and after an interminable time carried into a building and dumped upon the floor of a room whether at night or in the daytime I could not have told, as there was little or no light then or during the whole time I was there. So I lay on the floor, which seemed wet, for a time; and then finding my consciousness thoroughly I began to take cognizance of what lay near me.

A shiver of horror — that same dread — rushed over me instantly as I felt, in stretching out my hand, the body of a man. With a kind of spasmodic stroke of reason I felt at his heart, the dread growing as I could not find it beating, and in another moment I turned over and found him dead and cold. With the sort of movement which an insane man makes as he crouches away from something, I pushed myself across the floor eyeing the body, then whirled about in spite of the wound, for I touched something on the other side. 'T was another body. No! for it spoke.

" Have you a daughter, friend? " it asked.

" No," I whispered.

"Then take her and cut her throat, if you would keep her a virgin!"

"What mean you?" I asked, in strange awe, and, my eyes becoming accustomed to the darkness, I saw a haggard figure — naught but bones with the dried skin drawn tight over them — sitting Turk fashion and looking at me with wild eyes.

"Aye, cut her throat that she may live!"

"Where am I?" I asked to the air, for I became aware of a foul odour and sickening heavy atmosphere that, as it grew, made me try to stop breathing till it should pass; but that it did never.

"Don't min' 'im," said a gruff voice behind my head. "'E's *got* 'em! 'E's lifted, *'ere!* 'E's got a w'eel stuck in 'is upper deck."

I sat up quickly, holding my clothes now dried to the wound to keep from tearing them away from my side, and saw dimly a long narrow room with walls of stone and little slits for windows, with every inch of floor covered by standing or sitting men, so close together that in many instances they lay across one another. I had for the moment more room than the others.

"Where am I?"

"In hell! In hell!" cried the lunatic. "And she is not here. Will you cut her throat, friend?" I crawled away from him, fascinated by his unwinking eyes, till I touched the dead man.

"Give that un a wide berth, mate," said the sailor. "'E just coughed up 'is last breath, and 'e's got the typhus."

"Where am I?" I cried again, shrinking from the body.

"The lunatic's about right," said the sailor, in his monotonous voice. "Ye're in 'ell. D'yer mean to say yer don' know the old Sugar 'Ouse?"

God knows I did! And I hid my face in my hands to cover my grief. Did I know the Sugar House Prison, where my comrades of '77 had lain so long, some only leaving to go as I had seen them in the dead carts but a few hours before? Did I know that foul prison? Aye, well! And was like to know it better.

"What day is it?" asked a quiet voice at my feet. I turned a little and heard a long cough come from a young man pale with the signs of death on his white brow, lying there on his side, his quiet face resting on his arm, his eyes looking at me with a bravery in them that was pitiful, pitiful beyond measure!

"Thursday," said some voice out of the foul darkness.

"Wednesday," said I, as I instinctively turned towards the wasted figure.

"What month, if you please?" he asked, without taking his eyes from my face.

"The thirteenth of October, friend," said I.

He lay still a moment, looking at me without letting his gaze waver. Then:

"What year?"

"1780, comrade. Where do you belong?"

"'80," said he, thoughtfully, in the same voice.

"1780. I have been here two years and near three months."

"My God!"

A figure approached us through the thick air, stepping carefully over those lying down and passing among those who stood or sat up.

"I cannot get any, John, brother," said he to the dying man.

"Thank ye, Jake," he answered, never turning his gaze from my face, nor changing his look or position. I looked up and saw a face like his own, and saw, too, the man swallow suddenly, and heard him cry in a piteous tone:

"They will not give me any, not a drop to save him," and, turning to a grated door through which came the little light we had, he leaned over another sleeping figure and spoke to the guard standing with a musket over his shoulder.

"Will you not get me a little water for my brother?"

"There ain't none," said the man.

"He is dying, and but a little water would save him!"

"There ain't none," said the man in precisely the same voice as before.

"I'll give you a guinea for a glassful!" pleaded the wretched man, moving over one or two others to reach the barred door.

"There ain't none," came to him again exactly as before, as the guard walked away.

In a moment he was back by his brother's side, for the lad had been caught with a sudden and terrible fit of coughing that shook his whole frame, and then he rolled over on his back and lay with his arms out-stretched, staring with wide open eyes at the ceiling, his chest falling and rising in long straining breaths.

With a faint cry the other stepped to the bars and cried out down the corridor:

"Will you not give me an inch of candle, man?"

The guard returned slowly.

"My brother is dying there — there! Do you not see him? I cannot see his face. For God's sake give me a bit of candle to see him die!"

"There ain't none!" said the guard, and walked on.

Then the boy's body shook and strained upward in a strange inhuman fashion, as I have seen a fish on the sand gasp and swell for water in his gills. He turned his eyes towards his brother, tried to say something, and one hand made a faint move as if to lift itself. The brother caught the movement at once, and kneeling down took the hand and looked steadfastly in the lad's face, we others lying silently and watching them both. A grim set came into his jaw.

"It's all right, John," said he softly, but firmly. "It's all right, lad!" The eyes looked steadfastly at him. "Right, brother," cried he again. "Keep thy grip, lad!" And he took the other hand as the boy suddenly raised his head, opened his mouth for an instant, and sank gently back with his chin sunk into his chest and lay still — and died then and there.

"Now, if it please God," cried the other with quiet tears running down his sallow face, "if it please God that I ever get away alive, I'll be a most bitter enemy!"

And I lay back upon the floor and hid my face
in my hands.

Could it be? Could it be that but a day or two
ago I had passed this grim building? Could it be
that, almost in sight of its gray walls, I had sat and
eaten and drunk and been happy in that simple touch
of her foot beneath mine? Could it be so? It did
not seem possible. Could it be, too, that that genial
Baron Riedesel and the young boy prince and his
comrades knew aught of this? And yet why not?
Did not we up in Connecticut this two years know
this hell and the other hells swinging at their rotten
cables in the river, that held their crowds of living
and dying and dead?

I must get away from this scene! I could not stand
it. And so with severe pain I rose carefully and,
picking my way over and among the two hundred
and more men in that long narrow room, made for
one of the small windows. Each was crowded two
and three deep with silent figures clinging together
in the hot air, their faces touching cheek to cheek
and filling the lower space of the window. Each man
had his mouth open drawing in long breaths.

"Would you but let me get a whiff of air, friend?"
I asked one of those on the outer edge of the group.
But no sooner had I spoken than a voice behind me
said:

"That is not your group!"

I turned to him and he must have seen my bewilderment, for he asked:

"When did you come?"

"But just now, this morning."

"You do not know then that the room is divided into groups of six men, and that every ten minutes a group must change to allow another six to breathe the air."

"No, I did not know it," said I wearily. And then without interest, but without discourtesy, I was assigned to group No. 37. Turning again to him who had spoken first, I asked what group those men now by the window belonged to, and he told me 't was No. 28.

"Then I cannot get to the window for an hour and a half?"

"That is it, my friend."

"So be it. If these men who have been here so long can stand it, so can I." And I was about to lie down, feeling unable to stand and knowing another of those shivers was coming on, when the tramp of military feet sounded in the corridor and a hoarse voice cried:

"Turn out your dead! All hands turn out your dead!"

"A strange, intangible rustling sounded through the room, before so silent that it did not seem as if so many men could be housed there. Then the crowd rose, except those who could never rise again this side the grave, and with the same quiet, silent method that everything seemed to have in that fetid room — the lack of interest, the sombre, mirthless procedure, the same set faces with only one expression on them — with all this a few raised the eight or ten bodies and carried them to the two doors leading into the corridor.

I watched from across the room and saw the living carry the dead brother tenderly, quietly in his arms and without a word deliver him to two soldiers, who, one taking him by the feet and the other by the arm pits, carried him off down the corridor, to be thrown without covering or burial service into the trenches outside the breastworks, there to rot with thousands of others, good men and true all of them!

With the same quiet manner the others settled back in silence to sit or lie motionless, looking at nothing, thinking, thinking for hours, days, weeks at a time, without speaking; others to walk aimlessly about over and among their fellows. I lay close by the wall trying to get such air as I could, now and then frozen with chills and with the pangs of hunger gripping me. But no morsel of food came to us that day, and only by the generosity of a man with whom I talked had I a bit of foul bread and salt beef.

So came the night, without change except for a shade less light in the room. But I slept, as I had during the day, in a doze that seemed even to me wrong and unnatural, and when I woke, somewhere in the early hours, my face and body burned with a fever and the undressed wound gave me terrible pain.

I pitched about a while on a bit of straw I had got into my possession, and then, turning to one near me, said:

" Are you awake, my friend? "

" Always," said the other immediately.

" Do you know aught of the chirurgeon's work? "

"No, man, that I do not. What is it?"

"I have a wound here," answered I. "And if I could but get my clothes away from it, 'twould be less trouble."

"Let the cloth stick to it, lad," said he. "The room is full of typhus and smallpox, and 't were better to keep it closed. But wait till daylight when we can see it better."

So I lay wide awake for several hours till the light came slowly in, my thoughts running riot at times, so that I thought that I might go out of my head. And then I would go over every hour of my life with her, from the wet night and the broken coach-wheel to that moment at the prince's *soirée* when she turned from me and my heart died within me. It was all a matter of three short weeks, yet I could not fancy my existence before it, could not remember much of what I had thought or felt for twenty years. And then, fancy running on, I would present to myself, as one will, thousands of impossible "ifs."

If I had now the chance of going out freely into the open air and away from the city, but to do that must give up — must not know at all — my short three weeks with her, would I do it? And I knew in my heart that I would lie down on the dirty straw and shake my head. Yet how could she doubt me? What was she thinking, doing, feeling now, and now? And then what had become of Curtis and Acton and that foul specimen of manhood that went with them? What of the expedition towards Newport? And so back again to Deborah Philipse, and round her and

round her in a circle of thought, with the fever climb-
ing into my veins all night long.

At daybreak the guards came, bringing each man
six days' rations, and we were ordered to form in
line and march past, taking our share one by one.
When it came to my turn I found lying in my hand
about two pounds of raw pork and as much weight
of sea biscuit. And finding my friend, we got an
iron bucket wherewith one could heat the water. So
we cooked and ate our meal, saving only a bit of water
with which the kind friend helped me get my shirt
away from the wound. And then, tearing the linen
up into ribbons, he wound it tight around my body
for a bandage.

As he did so, his eye brightened a bit.

"I knew a queer bird up the river who was part
chirurgeon and part man of God — though mostly
pirate," said he, "who showed me how thus to tie a
bandage." I paid little heed to what the man said,
for just then a faintness from the pain took me. "He
knew somewhat of all three trades. A strange beast
was old Marvin! I wonder if he is hung yet?" and
he smiled quietly to himself.

"Marvin," said I, suddenly, "where?"

"Up above Tarrytown in the neutral country. I
was there myself —"

"Marvin, say you, man?" cried I, again. "What
sort?"

"A sober villain; solemn of face, but with the
capacity for gallons of good ale — but why? Do you
know him?"

"Aye, well! But is he then of a fact a minister of the church?" and my wound and the old prison were forgotten as I waited for his answer.

"True enough! Though, God knows, he does more honour to hell and its king — the devil."

"Marvin — Jim Marvin?"

"Aye, lad, old Jim Marvin! You can see him any day at Gowan's Tavern — What is it? Is the cut paining ye?"

The cut! What pain could touch me just then? Pain or no pain, dead or alive, one thing was sure. There lived no longer on this earth a Deborah Philipse. But a Deborah there was — aye, should I ever see her again?

So the days passed on, one like another, except that the heat ended and gradually the cold came on, first a comfort to us all, then disagreeable, and finally terrible. For we had no sign of fire, except perhaps once a week for our water boiling. This, too, stopped when, as I inferred, the want of wood in the town took what little we were before allowed.

This cold got into my never healing wound and I began to grow too weak to stand at all, and was so sitting against the wall one day, close to some new-made friends, that we might keep one another warm, when some forty new prisoners arrived; and I, lying back with my head to the wall and my eyes closed, heard one telling some of my companions that he came from Tappan.

"When, man?" I asked, leaning forward quicker than I thought I could.

" But three days ago."

" Tell me then if you can, back two months now, about the middle of October, did Clinton move on Newport? "

" That he did, but got no further than Huntington Harbour with all his forces."

" Why, man, why? " I asked.

" Why, because the Commander-in-Chief, by some means I do not know, got wind of the thing before it started and made a feint — I was with my command, and 't was a stiff fight, too — on Staten Island and at Paulus' Hook, and back came scurrying the Johnnies with their tails between their legs, thinking the town was taken or going soon to be."

" Thank God," I muttered to myself, lying back again as the man went rambling on. Curtis and Acton must be safe, then. And Hazeltine, too, dead or alive! After all, we had not done so ill, and I had kept my word to the general so far as man could. But I knew I must be weak indeed, for the excitement of the new man's story had taken the life out of me, and I slid down to the cold floor all in a sweat that drenched my clothes and then froze upon them.

With that I sank back into a quiet stupor that lasted I know not, nor never knew, how long; but happier than I had thought to be since coming to the Sugar House. From time to time, as I waked a bit and looked about, I would catch two or three comrades looking down at me as I lay not uncomfortably on a little clump of straw, and, seeing me looking at them, they would ask me how I did. And I smiled

and told them, truthfully, as well as they. Once a
young and big fellow took his coat and threw it over
me, and, try as I would, I could not make him take
it back; for just then I could not seem to rise up on
my elbow, and by and by I laughed and thanked him
and turned aside and slept long, I know not how
long.

So I awoke once and found it light in the old house,
for the snow reflected on the ceiling; and seeing the
group, larger than before, standing about me I asked
for a bit of water, and it came to my lips at once.
Some one I heard talking quietly and looking at me,
and I caught the word "going." And I remember
thinking then with some interest that perhaps there
was a rumour of our going out of this frozen hell.
And on asking if 't was so, they said in their same un-
emotional way, "Yes, man, some of us — some of
us will go shortly."

Then on a sudden the group slipped away, why I
could not see, till I caught the glint of red uniforms
and saw an officer and some men walking about the
room stopping now and then. I lay so on my side
idly watching them approach, when the blood froze
in my veins.

'T was Captain Atherton moving quietly along,
pointing now and then to a prisoner. He must not
see me! That I knew; and so I shrank back into my
straw and waited in a kind of terror to see if he would
get by. So he came on slowly, so slowly, looking at
each and every man and saying not a word. But as
he pointed to a prisoner that one was lifted and car-

ried out. I could not keep my eyes from him. And then he came by me.

On a sudden he stepped back. Then quickly muttering that he had slipped, I saw him point at me and walk on, still studying each man. Two soldiers leaned down and took me up gently enough, for I felt no pain; and then we passed down the corridor, down the stairs and into a light room. There stood Atherton and pointed to a couch, where they laid me and passed out, and I turned my face to the wall, in hopes he had not recognised me. But in truth the couch being soft and comfortable I did not much care, but gave something of a long sigh and — went to sleep.

CHAPTER XXIII

'TWAS but a moment when I opened my eyes
again, and with that came the dread of seeing Atherton there in the office of the prison,
looking at me. So that I lay quite still and listened.
No sound came to me, but I knew in the sleepy way
I had acquired of late that there was a bright light
there, and that I was warm and so comfortable as
I had not been these two months. But strange that
I could not move! My side was as stiff as a board,
so stiff that I softly and carefully raised my arm and
felt — not the sofa, but straw.

And then came a sickening consciousness that I
was back in the prison house. I picked up a bit of
straw, but it felt soft and would not yield to my
pulling, and looking down I had like to have cried
out when I saw in my hand a white and spotless
counterpane.

Perfectly quiet I lay, my mind working so fast
that it pained me sorely. Over my head I saw a roof,
and then, quick and fast, came the knowledge that I
lay on a great bed with four posts supporting a roof
hung with silken curtains. I tried to move, and
found, though I had no pain, that the wound was too

stiff to allow me to turn, and, putting my hand to
my side, it met tight cloth bandages that ran around
me from groin to armpits, and then up over either
shoulder and around my neck.

There I lay with eyes shut, and thought and
thought. What could it be? Was I — could it be —
could I be losing my mind, and should I begin to
ask if some one would cut my daughter's throat?
Then I bade myself be quiet, and held myself tense
to see — to think — to realise the reality. But it
would not do, I could not bear it, and cried out:

" Where am I ? "

That instant the curtain was pulled back and I
saw a face looking at me. Then on the moment
't was gone. And I fancied I heard the soft rustle
of a gown as the figure flew out through the room.
Was it Atherton? I strained my weak head to think,
to decide. I could not tell. It must be, and yet —
and yet it did not seem to be so, and the face that
it resembled — aye! my mind was gone stark mad.
'T was the face it could never be!

So I lay, turning a bit to one side that I might
see the door as it stood open into a hall with the
sunlight playing across the floor and dancing upon
the polished furniture. Gradually I was straining
myself out of a mist of thoughts, when there came
a rustle, and two little faces peeped in at me, and
I not moving, they came on through the door — two
little faces hung about with fair curls, one of golden
brown and one of black, and carried on little shoulders and little bodies dressed in white gowns.

"*She sits here all day and every night, always*"

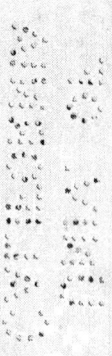

There could be no doubt of it, — angels they might be, but they were two little girls of some four or five summers. I waved my hand weakly to them, and asked them to come and talk to me. My voice had a strange and pitifully jaded sound, and the smile that ran over my face seemed to crack the skin by the unaccustomed wrinkles it created.

"Come here, children," mumbled I, "and tell me who was here but now."

They sidled up, holding tight to one another's hands, the chubby little fairy hanging back, both looking at me with great startled eyes through the fringes of curls — startled, but filled with curiosity, too.

"Who was here but now, little ones?" I asked again.

"Tante. She sits here all day and every night always," said the older, opening her eyes wide.

"And the *Lieber Gott*," said the chubby one.

"And who?"

"The *Lieber Gott*. Tante says He is here with you all the time, too."

"Yeth, all the time," said the chubby one. "But we can't catch him."

"We've tried every day," said the other, as they began to grow confidential.

"Yeth," said Chubby. "We've twied evwy day."

"We thought we had found him once."

"Yeth, we thought we'd found him once," repeated little Echo, "but 'twas a wat scwatchin', Tante said."

I lay back thanking God for I knew not what.

"And who is Tante?" I asked, softly.

They looked at one another and took a new grip on their hands.

"She's just Tante," said the older, standing on the other white-socked foot.

"Yeth, juth Tante," said Echo.

"And who are you?"

"We're mudder's dears," said the older, simply, as she came to my bedside.

"God knows you are!" cried I, weakly, and the tears rolled out of my eyes because I had no power to stop them. I had to wait a moment, and then:

"Will you lean over and give me a kiss?" and she did, but Chubby could not reach and had to forego.

"Is He here?" she asked confidentially.

"Who?"

"The *Lieber Gott*. Tante says He will cure you."

"I think He must be. I hope—" But I could not go on. Weakness—absurd weakness without pain, simply a lack of power—stopped me, and just then, closing my eyes, I heard the rustle of a dress and an anxious, nay, terrified whisper, saying:

"Children, children, what have you done? Haven't I told you never to come in here? Where is Tante?"

"Thhe wan away and the *Lieber Gott* did, too," said Chubby.

"So we came in," said the older.

"Sh!" said the whisper again. "Run away at once," and as they trotted off, the curtains drew aside and I opened my eyes, still with the tears in

them, and smiled straight into the beautiful face of
the Baroness Riedesel.

"Where am I?" I asked weakly.

She put her finger to her mouth and raised her
eyebrows.

"Do you know me?" she asked. "Don't speak.
Just nod."

I nodded.

"Are you perfectly conscious?"

I nodded.

She moved away, and I cried out and asked her
where I was.

"You must not talk or move till I get the doctor.
You are in our house in New York."

"How long —" I could not finish, but made a
gesture towards the bed.

"Nearly six weeks ago you were brought here,"
and she was gone, still with her finger on her lips.

I lay back in wonder, and though weak I felt
strong, though ill I felt well. I cannot tell how it
was, but I settled all the muscles of my body down
upon the soft bed and took as long a breath as my
bandages would allow. So I lay I know not how
long, and the door opened quickly but silently and
in came the sharp face of Dr. Low, followed by the
baroness. Silently they came on. Silently he drew
up a chair and sat, taking my hand, while she stood
behind him looking over his shoulder.

"So, young man," said Low, cheerily. "You're
looking round a bit. So! So!" he went on, looking
at his watch. "So! open your mouth!" I did.

"Stick out your tongue. So, not so bad! Now drink that," and down went something, I all the while looking at him in wonder.

Apparently the baroness misunderstood my look, for she said hastily, but softly:

"Do not fear the doctor! He will not betray you. He is only here to cure you."

At that, Low, sitting thus with his back to her and looking at me, closed one eye slowly without the changing of another muscle of his face and as slowly opened it again, and I could have laughed aloud, but I asked:

"Who is Tante?" I do not know what I thought. I could not let myself believe or hope anything, but I must ask, and know and get it over with. The baroness smiled at me, and Low said in a tone that meant nothing:

"Oh, she's an old hag we hired here to nurse you."

"I think you lie, Doctor," said I weakly, and looked at the baroness. She nodded brightly, and I made an involuntary movement.

"Here! here!" cried Low. "Perhaps I do lie, but do you lie still and go promptly to sleep."

"I cannot."

"Yes, you can! Why, man, you've got one foot and three quarters of the other in the grave still. Off you go!" And he got up and took the baroness by the arm and walked out of the room closing the door.

Sleep! How could I sleep? Who was she? Might it be? Six weeks. What was the matter with me?

And so I lay and thought and thought, and then — the door slowly opened. I looked and saw a head, a face and a bit of white gown.

It was she! And I stretched out my sickly hand to her and made some silly gurgling sound and — she was gone instantly and the door again shut.

And then and there, I, Merton Balfort, lay over on my back and looked up at the canopy of the bed above me — and thanked God at some length! And so I slept long, and waked again stronger and fresher by much than before, and as I moved in my bed there came the setting aside of the curtains again, the rustle of a dress, and there she stood looking at me, for an instant. But as I moved she was gone, and I began to lose my temper and ask myself what was the matter, and, as a sick man will, complained of my fate.

Then I took counsel with myself, and turning to one side, so that I could see the door, I thrust one arm under the pillow, put my head down so that I covered one eye but left the other free, and then, with some labour, be it acknowledged, placed the other arm over my face, with but a small opening left for the one eye to watch the door. Then I lay quiet, as if again asleep.

'T was a long time, and I began to lose my small stock of nerve, when the door again slid open a bit and her head appeared cautiously. Seeing me thus asleep, she came slowly on tiptoe with a look in her face that lives with me always, and the quiet rustle of her gown. And so coming near, she knelt down

by the bed, the proud white neck bent forward and
her brown head resting in her hands on the counterpane close to me. And there she lay quietly for a
long while, till suddenly the curls began to quiver
and the shoulders to shake, and to my wonder I
heard a soft sob, then another, then another. I
could bear it no longer and quietly raising my arm
I put my hand on her head.

" Deborah ! "

She was half across the room in an instant, looking
at me in terror, with her hands clasped at her breast
and tears in her eyes.

" Are you awake ? " she asked in a whisper.

" Yes, Deborah," said I, " and I am very tired.
Will you not come and fix my pillow for me ? "

She was by me in an instant, rearranging something that was already right, murmuring again and
again as she did so, " My dear, my dear, my dear,"
as she pushed back the hair from my forehead,
straightened the counterpane and brought me something to drink — still murmuring "My dear, my dear,"
in feverish haste, silently, for all the world like a
quiet worried angel.

" Deborah ! "

" You must not talk ! you must not say a word,"
she cried out under her breath, putting her hand
gently over my mouth. And suddenly she knelt
again by the bedside and laid her head close to
mine, her face buried in the pillow, and I could hear
her still murmuring, " My dear ! my dear ! I 'm so
sorry, so sorry, so sorry ! "

A sudden fear seized me, and I pushed myself instinctively away from her and tried to speak. Some sound made her look up and she cried out in a frightened tone:

"What is it?"

"What is the matter with me? Is it — ?"

"No, no, 't was the brain fever. Dr. Low says 't was a miracle you had not the smallpox. Aye, dear," she went on, seeing my face, "let us both thank God." And a cool hand was laid on my forehead. I kept still a moment, my eyes closed for very weakness, and then, with some struggle, I got my arms up to my head and took her hand and put it to my lips. She was on her feet again, all changed in a moment, and stood by me looking away and saying not a word. She might have drawn her hand away, for I had not the strength to hold it, but there it lay, trembling like herself, much as a little tame bird might lie an instant in your hand, half for comfort staying, half for fear ready to fly. So I stroked it, and laid it to my hot cheek, and kissed it again, and looked up at her standing over me.

"Dear, will you forgive me?"

For answer she started a little, the colour flying over her face; and then she stooped and lightly kissed me and flew out of the room.

The thought of losing her was too much for me and I yelled out a savage cry that brought her back in terror, saying that I would die if I lay not still.

"Then stay here!" I said hoarsely. "If you go away I — I will get out of bed!" Though God

knows I could not have sat up to save my life.
"Come close to me — and — and talk." Something
in my face must have drawn her, for she came and
lay upon the counterpane, and lifting my head put
it upon her arm. And so she talked, her fair head
close to mine, whispered quietly such words as I
would no more put to paper, even if I could, than
I would tell the thoughts of my inmost soul to any
one but God. No one can be held to speak of this
one hour of his life. It is his for all time and only
his, his to think on in after years, in times of stress
and trouble, to dream on year by year! And it shall
go out to no other, for it is true and sacred and
belongs to him alone.

So thus I lay, closing my eyes from weakness and
comfort, yet must I quickly open them again, because
I could look at her close by me and feared she would
again be gone. And by and by something in her
words set my head a-going, and looking at her I
asked, scarcely by means of words, how I came there.

"I did not know, dear! We thought you gone. I
dared not ask. No one gave me a hint, till one day
came a messenger to me from my brother in his
camp, asking if you were dead and saying where
and how they left you." And for a space she could
not go on; till, looking again, I saw a far-off light
in the depths of her eyes, different from anything I
had yet read there. I have said it a dozen times
here, yet must I say it again: Never have I looked
into such eyes, so different with every flying mood,
so much a tell-tale of her thoughts.

"And then I caught one evening at dinner a hint that finally led to my hearing from his own lips of Captain Atherton's — of your — your — dear! My dear! — of that morning at Corlear's Hook." Again she lay still. Again I opened my eyes and she went on: "He had such a strong, manly respect, such a chivalrous remembrance of you that I came to like him and trust him, and told him of Robert's letter, and begged him to learn something of you. And that day he began going through every prison ship, every place where men were confined, on the plea of selecting those who had smallpox. And each night he would come to me with a sorrowful shake of his head, but hopeful words and never a fear or complaint of the danger he ran.

"No record could be found of your name. You seemed to have sunk into the earth. Then he tried to tell me gently that he believed you dead. I could not hear him and begged, besought him to go again through the prisons. I asked Sir Henry to let me go and nurse the sick, that I might look for you. But he would not hear of it, and only laughed at me for a quixotic miss."

I stroked the hand that lay in mine gently, and she went on.

"So one day I was sitting here in this house — indeed, the good baroness brought me here and kept me with her constantly — when Captain Atherton came to us running up the street and cried that he had found you, and how, and that you were very ill, and Dr. Low was already gone to see if you — your

life — might yet be saved! Dear, can you think what
that hour of waiting was to me? I sat here by the
window, while, as I learned afterwards, this best of
friends told the captain to have you brought to her
own house — even when she did not know if you
might not have the dreadful plague — and told the
captain all your story, for I had told her.

"And he, finding that the doctor said you had
nothing contagious, so far as he could see, though
you were nearly dead from fever and lack of food —
he brought you here in a cart covered with straw
and vegetables to conceal you. And that was over
six weeks gone now! And God, the good God be
thanked for to-day, when you opened your eyes and
I saw reason there for the first time!"

The brown head came close to mine and lay quietly
except for the shake of a sob now and then, which
she tried in vain to suppress. And I, what of me?
Will not a man yet complain of heaven? There I
lay cursing my illness, for that I was too weak to
take her in my arms, and could do naught but turn
my useless head to one side and put my lips to the
white sleeve that supported me.

Soon I pressed her hand, and she looked at me. I
wanted to ask much and knew not how, but only said:

"Curtis?"

"My brother?" said she. "You would know how
he is?"

I nodded.

"Safe and sound in his camp at Verplancks. He
got away in a boat across the river."

"Acton?"

"Yes, he too, Rob says, is well and safe."

Then I looked at her steadily and said not a word. And she sat up and got upon the floor, with sorrow in her face and something like dread written there, too.

"I cannot tell you," she whispered, standing over me. "Some one else must do it. I cannot! I cannot!"

"Oh," said a gruff voice behind her, "oh, go right on! Don't mind me! Kill him, kill him! Egad, ma'am, why don't you take him for a walk and give him truffles and champagne? Aye! don't look at me, and plead and tell me this and that! Just bang him on the head. He's good and strong, and should be thrown out on the snow!"

'T was Low, going on in sarcastic wrath, and she had run to him with consternation in her eyes.

"Ah, Doctor, Doctor, have I done wrong? He said he would get up and follow me if I left him."

"Get up!" snorted Low. "And how the devil, ma'am, think you, he is going to get up? Look now! his cheeks are all red again! Aye, and here 's fever. Why, you young reprobate of a nurse, have I taught ye these two months so poorly as this?"

"Oh, Doctor!" cried she, in real alarm.

"Tut! not a word! But run and get him some of the milk and wine and a bit of rennet —" and she was gone in a flash.

"Well, lad," said he at that. "Ye'll fight again, eh? How do you find yourself?" And he brought a bottle of some nasty liquid and poured part of it into a spoon.

"I need none of your bad tasting stuff," said I, trying to laugh.

"Oho," said he. "No nasty stuff! I suppose you 've been having that that tastes better than good iron, eh? Well, well, lad," and his voice changed, "'t is the best medicine God could send ye. But remember you 've no more backbone in you than a bit of cake, and go not too far. Here," he added. "Look at that!" and he held a little mirror before my eyes.

And if truth be told, 't was a wretched-looking man that gazed out at me, with a great black growth of beard covering my crooked features, with hollow eyes gazing out of a sunken, sallow-skinned visage that gave me a start to think on.

"A nice pirate," said he again, "eh? to be going on talking and fandangling with pretty girls. Ah! Mistress Debby! Bring it here, and go and lock yourself up in the garret, young woman." But I would not have it and swore I would not eat till she gave it me herself. And so, grumbling as he did with a twinkle in his eye, she sat down on the bedside and fed me with a spoon and said not a word; but then what mattered it since I could look at her and she at me? When I had done she went away again and I asked Low the question I could not put to her. His face clouded at once.

"Dead, lad. Dead before they got him to Paulus' Hook. Bob Philipse wrote to her and told her. 'T is a good riddance, for there never was a fouler friend nor foe than Frank Pendleton."

My head sank back upon the pillow, and the sweat came out on my face as I ran over the night again.

"Let it not worry thee, lad," went on the doctor gently. "I know the whole tale from another source than Philipse's letter. You drowned a rat, that's all. Now get ye to sleep, and when you wake up again, you'll be a hundred per centum the stronger."

So he left me alone, and I lay watching the door for some one else, but before she came I had done his bidding.

CHAPTER XXIV

A CASE OF "NONE BUT THE BRAVE"

'TIS wonderful what a day of sleep will do to a man. When I awoke and found Low— 't was high noon next day — ready to take off my bandages and dress my wound, I would for awhile sit up, and did so. And after he had strapped me up again the baroness came in with my breakfast, and, noting something in my face, apologised for herself as a nurse, saying that my real nurse was out for an airing with Captain Atherton — which, to tell good truth, but irritated me — and that shortly she would return. I told her of my gratitude for her kindness — more than kindness — to me, and she would have it that 't was not for me at all, but only on behalf of Mistress Debby that I was there.

"The dear girl began to grow ill after the night you disappeared," said she. "Something, I knew not what, was gnawing at her heart. And when her brother's letter came she was nearly frantic with grief, and came then and told me much that I had guessed before. Then came Captain Atherton to her aid — and you owe much to him. We are not all," she added, smiling sadly, "we are not all tyrants and villains, you see."

"You are more than kind friends," I said seriously.

"You and the captain are risking your lives to help an enemy."

She laughed again.

"'T was but to save a young chit's life," said she. "Of course we cared naught for you."

"You are good and kind, dear lady, beyond comprehension," I answered, and she gave me her hand frankly. "And your little daughters brought me back to the world in a way I shall never forget."

"They are nearly as bad as Debby," said she, with the pleasure showing in her face that always came there when she spoke of her children. "We could do naught with Debby. Day by day she sat here by you and watched and listened to your dreadful ravings, and heard you crying out at her cousin, and then calling on her name, telling her in a vibrant voice" — and she smiled, though she seemed still startled at the remembrance of it — "the particular place she held in your affections, which men usually whisper, I hear, in the silence of solitude."

"Did I do so?" I asked.

"For twenty-four hours in the day, week after week, and I have seen her sitting here looking at you as if her heart would break, wringing her hands and begging Dr. Low to make you hear her and understand."

"What can I ever do for her to repay half, or for you either? I wonder that she kept her health?"

"Once we tried to get her away," she continued. "And by Dr. Low's orders she went to her room. But in the night your cries nearly drove her mad, and,

19

though the doctor said 't would undermine her health, I went to her, and she begged me on her knees to let her go in to you, and — and — " smiling brightly, "and she asked me how would I feel if the baron were ill and I shut in another room away from him! That was a shrewd little argument."

The tears stood in her eyes and in mine, too. What had the girl not done for me, with never a word of explanation from me to set her mind at rest?

"Where is she?" I asked, a little huskily. "Why does she not come to me?"

With a laugh the baroness got up, and saying that we were apparently a pair, went in search of her. But she did not come and the day waned. The bright afternoon faded to sundown, and still she did not come. Some one brought in lamps and at last the baroness appeared with an amused, yet puzzled look in her face.

"Is she not coming to say good night to me?" I asked.

"I do not quite understand her," said she. " Poor girl, she's tired and worried."

"What is it?" I asked again. "Is there something wrong?"

She smiled again.

"I think she is a little afraid," said the baroness.
" I — "

"Afraid? Afraid of what?" I asked.

"Well, I scarcely know," she answered again. "I — " and then, leaning over to me, "Shall I tell you a dreadful secret about women?"

I looked at her in amazement.

"I think — I am afraid —" Then she stopped, and a pretty flush went over her face. "I'm afraid women like — a — little masterful treatment!" And, as I am a sinner, off she went like any young girl with the fires on her cheeks.

I lay back in my bed an instant, and then called her back.

"Dear baroness," I said, "will you enter a little conspiracy with me?"

She nodded brightly.

"I shall be very ill again," said I. "And shall shriek some more. Will you chance to pass by with — ?"

"Do you happen to have any idea, young man, where she has been these three hours?"

I had not the least, unless out walking with Captain Atherton.

"She is sitting just outside that door by the window in the hall."

I simply signed to her to begin the conspiracy, and she passed out, leaving the door ajar. I waited a moment and then began to talk, and rambled on, getting louder and louder, till finally I yelled out a lot of idiotic nonsense putting in her name. Then I paused and heard through the doorway much whispering, and howled again, hearing in a moment, "Oh what is it? Can it be true? Again?" That voice hit my conscience hard, but I yelled out again. Whereupon the door opened and in she came running to me and speaking my name softly and taking my hand.

In a moment I had her fast by the arm.

"Where have you been all day, madam?"

She stood back, looking at me in wonder, but she could not escape.

"Sit down, dear heart," said I. "Sit down, sit down. 'T was all a conspiracy to get you in here."

Then I thought she would be angry, but with a flush she said:

"I am too relieved to be offended, but 't was not fair, was it?"

"No, dear, 't was a cowardly trick. But Deborah!"

Down went the face and the eyes looked around the floor, as she sat by my bed.

"Debby, look at me."

The eyes never moved.

"Deborah, is it necessary for me, sitting here done up in five miles of rags, too absurdly weak to stand up — is it necessary for me to make love to you?" Up came the eyes straight at me with some of the old fearless fire in them. "Do you want me to ask you to marry me?"

There was an instant's silence and then she suddenly gave way to a burst of merry laughter.

"It seems to me, sir," with a toss of her head, "that you put your question a bit late in the day, since we have been married now some six months."

That sobered me, for I remembered that I knew something still unknown to her, and sitting there by the light of the lamp I told her of the comrade who had helped me in the Sugar House, and what he knew of Marvin.

For a moment she sat quietly looking away from
me, her hands lying in her lap. Then, turning to
me with a depth in her beautiful eyes that seemed
so new and recent, she gently laid her hand in mine
and sat there looking at me without a word for minute
after minute; till I leaned forward and took her fair,
serious face in my two hands and drew it toward me
and kissed it once, twice, and asked:

"Are you happy, Deborah?"

"Yes, dear," said she, simply. —

"Well, what the devil do I care, madam? I've
got to dress the man's wound. Egad, they can't
bill and coo twenty-four hours in the day. Let me
in!" This from the other side of the door. A
whispered pleading was his answer.

"Not at all! He can't get up till he's well. So
in I go. " And in he came, puffing and fuming, and
unwound and wound me up again.

It was as he was rewinding the bandages after
dressing the wound that the door opened and Atherton came in. Up he strode to me, with something
of a shamefaced look and shook hands.

"How are ye, old man," said he, as if he had seen
me and talked but yesterday.

"Right and fit, friend," said I, and then we fell
to silence. 'T is ever a strange thing to me, and yet
something I cannot fail to like, to see, as I did now,
two Anglo-Saxons trying to hide all the good feelings in them. Even Low laughed out as he worked
on and said:

"What's the price of beer?"

"'Gad! I'd like some now, eh, Balfort?" cried
Atherton, and, growing easier, he sat down and
watched the skilful hands of the doctor. I stretched
out and took his hand.

"Captain," said I, "you've done more for me than
any —"

"Tut, tut, man," cried he, wringing my poor weak
hand till it ached. "Not a word! 'T was nothing.
Let it pass. Doctor, for God's sake give us a drink!
Is there naught of alcohol in this house?"

"Drink, you big fool!" cried Low. "Do you want
to kill him?"

"Oh, he's fit to fight again, and show me what a
man can do besides fight."

"Look ye here, Atherton," said I seriously. "I'm
your prisoner. What will you do with me?"

"Hell!" said he. "Let's talk of something
pleasanter."

"That I will not, man," I answered. "I must get
away and you cannot let me go."

He looked at me an instant, and I knew the same
thought had been in his mind since he heard I could
recover.

"Balfort," he said in a moment, "will you give me
your parole till the end of the war?"

I knew it long before he said it, and leaning back
on my pillow, I told him I could not.

"Give ye his parole, you raving idiot," cried Low
— never was such an actor lived as that same chirurgeon. "Why, look, man! look!" and with that he
unwound the bandages he had begun to replace and

laid bare the wound. I looked down at it and my gorge rose at the sight. 'T was a slit, a ragged cut from my right hip up along the ribs near to my shoulder, a good twelve inches. Only by the grace of chance was it that Hazeltine's point had not caught on a rib and gone through me. And the edges stood even now far apart and ugly and irregular.

" Parole?" went on the doctor. " Why, man, he cannot hold a sword for a year! "

Atherton looked at it and took my hand again.

" Friend," said he, " will ye give me your parole for six months? To tell ye the truth, your army cannot hold out that long, and I am safe."

By chance I caught the doctor's eye, and knew in some way that he bade me accept it, so, lying back again, I told Atherton I would.

" Then I get you out of here when you can move."

Again I gave him my hand and thanked him till he swore he 'd hear no more and went off with Low.

And so the days passed on, quickly enough for a matter of three weeks. And then, beginning to feel stronger, I commenced to fret and worry and wonder when I would get away and what was happening at West Point, and where were my companions in Putnam's division, and what of Curtis — or Philipse, as I should call him — and Acton. I was up now and walking over the house, but not allowed to go out. I talked with Low when we were alone about the best way of going, and he had a plan all arranged. But I had another that was worth ten of his, for that it had another purpose, which I could only talk over with

one other person, and that one the baroness. Her
husband had been away all the time in the South
with his Germans, and so I saw much of her — much
of every one, in fact, except Mistress Debby, who
would talk with me less and less.

So one day I broached my plan to the good lady.
At first she said 't would be impossible, and then, her
eyes shining, she said I should do it, if she could
bring it about. And we began the scheme by her telling my proud mistress that I was shortly going away.

When next I got a word with her, we had but just
finished tea and were walking in the great drawing-
room, she and I. I saw how silent she was, and with
some misgivings began:

"Deborah."

"Yes?"

"Deborah, soon I must get back to my camp," said
I, gently.

"You cannot go! You would not go, would you?"
cried she. "You are not well enough. Will you leave
me?"

"I am quite well now," I answered, as quietly as
I could.

"You are not! you are not!" she murmured, taking
hold of my arm and looking at me. "You could not
stand the dreadful camp life."

"I must, dear. I cannot waste my life here."

"Waste?" said she, slowly.

"You know well what I mean."

She sat down then, and I by her, and naught was
said for a while.

"I cannot let you go!" said she, presently.

"There's one way out of it," said I.

Up came her troubled face and looked at me.

"Will you come with me?"

The fair face set, and the eyes looked straight into mine.

"I would go anywhere in the world with you. But what could you do with me in a camp?"

"What did the Baroness Riedesel in her castle in Germany, when her husband left her for a camp three thousand miles across the sea?"

"And brought her children with her, too," she murmured. Then, looking up, she added hastily, "I do not fear to go, believe me, dear."

"I never once thought you did." And the baroness coming in then, she ran to her and threw her arms around her neck and kissed her. I stood by a moment, and then the little lady turned towards me, laid her two hands in mine, and, looking at me and at the baroness, she said:

"I'll go gladly. Wilt take me?"

"Aye, that I will, Debby dear, and God bless your brave heart. 'T will be a different life from this, and you do not like the cause."

"'T is yours and shall be mine. And 't is Robert's too."

"We have a little plan," said the baroness to her, "Merton and I. You shall be married here in this house, and Captain Atherton will get you out."

"Oh!" cried the brazen minx. "I think I'll go as I am."

" What! " cried the baroness.

" I 'm married enough now," quoth the lady with a twinkle in her eye.

" You naughty girl! " said the scandalised matron again.

" 'T is but a form," said Deborah, " and I 'm satisfied now."

" *Lieber Herr Je*," cried the horrified baroness, raising her hands and looking at the girl in amazement.

I could stand it no longer, but must spoil all by laughing.

" What have you two in your heads? " asked the mystified lady.

" Naught but this, ma'am," said Mistress Deborah, and with a sweeping courtesy she took 'from her bodice a paper and handed it to the astonished matron.

'T was now my turn to be astonished, and going to the baroness, I looked over her shoulder, and read the scrawling signature of " James Marvin, Minister of the Gospel," and Deborah's and mine, and the statement above them. Then I turned to her with something rising in my throat:

" You have kept this all the time? " I asked.

She nodded.

" And you would not let me keep it? " I asked again.

" No, sir! for I valued it more than you."

" That you did not, madam! nor half as much, then! " said I, defiantly.

" That I did, good sir! and fifty times as much *then!* " said she, with a courtesy.

"Children! children!" cried the baroness, "stop your bickering, and tell me what in heaven's name this means."

So we sat her down between us and told her, with much more "bickering," as she called it, the only part of the story she had not already heard.

CHAPTER XXV

"WELL, madam, you seem greatly pleased with yourself," said I, a week later, as we rode two staunch beasts northward towards Tarrytown.

"Thank you, sir, I am quite at my ease. I trust that your highness is pleased with me," and Debby looked across at me with a species of self-contained smile from under the hood, or cap, or whatever the thing she wore was called. It was this self-same smile, which I had noted throughout the day and which seemed to conceal something, that made me put the query.

"Madam," said I, "I have the honour to love your ladyship, and it would be difficult for you to displease me at the moment."

"Do not be so sure, Monsieur Merton! You have a very bad temper, as I —"

"Oh, have I?"

"Yes, now that I think of it, you have frequently treated me atrociously."

"When, if it please you?"

"Well, once on a time, when a certain wayward maiden —"

"Wayward maiden! I should think so —"

"When a certain wayward maiden asked a churlish horseman to help her from her broken coach, and he started to ride away —"

"Ah, but Debby dear, I did not know you then!"

"There is no question of that just now."

"Well?"

"Again, when some one, being but a weak and shy girl —"

"God save the mark! Good again! Weak and fiddlesticks!"

"When a very shy maiden objected to having a highwayman climb in at her chamber window —"

"Not at all!" said I, for that was still a sore point. "Not at all! 'T was the hall window, in the first place; and, furthermore, I would have you to know, Debby, that you might have recognised an honest man, and believed, too, that I would never have intruded myself upon you, had it not been for your own good."

"If I mistake not," said she, with a sweet and innocent smile, "some great lord said but a moment ago that he had no temper and could not be irritated by —"

"I said just so," I persisted, in truth a bit disturbed by the innocent demeanour I knew now so well. "But it is not fair to throw such things in my face!"

She doubled up in the saddle and laughed merrily for a moment; and then, looking up at me, she said:

"Merton, dear, if you could but look at that great serious face of yours once in the while, you would certainly die of laughing."

302 ♥ NONE BUT THE BRAVE — ♥

"My face, Mistress Deborah, is no doubt —"

But she turned her horse suddenly towards me and put her little gloved hand over my mouth.

"You stupid! Never tell me I cannot anger you! Dost not know, sir, that I shall have to spend all the time you have off duty teaching you some kind of a sense of humour? Why, Merton, my friend, I could make you so mad in two seconds that you would jump up and down and kick the furniture, and doubtless draw that huge sword of yours and brandish it over my head."

"Come here, madam, and I will chastise your disrespectful mouth now," and I turned towards her. But she sent her nag kiting ahead at a gallop, and I started hot in pursuit — angry, pleased, and above all, so happy with her for my companion that I forgot all else — forgot our present position, until I saw a British soldier step into the road ahead of us and call her to a halt. I was by her side in an instant; and, giving my passes to the picket, followed him into the guardhouse of the Tarrytown outpost.

As we turned into the same room where I had had so narrow an escape but a few months before, a familiar voice cried out: "How de do, Captain Hazeltine" — and I turned with a start to see the officer called Majoribanks, who had been so muddled on that memorable day. He took the passes as a matter of course, and as he read said:

"You look ill, Captain; somewhat thinner than when I saw you —" Then his eye caught what he was reading, and he stopped. "Mistress Deborah

Philipse," he read aloud, "and Captain Merton!
What is this, sir?"

I was on the point of replying, when Debby plucked
him by the sleeve and made a sign with her head to
signify that he was to send the picket out of the room.
He seemed to understand; and when we were alone
she spoke before I could get in a word.

"Captain Hazeltine goes frequently under assumed
names, sir, by special orders."

"Oh," said the officer, somewhat doubtfully, still
fingering the papers. Then I bethought me, and took
out the pass given me by the Commander-in-Chief.

"Here's the old one, Captain, if it be of any use to
you."

"Quite right, Captain! Quite right! Pardon my
hesitation. But, to be frank with you, several men
escaped — prisoners, you understand — but a day or
so ago on stolen passports, and I had a reprimand
from General Patterson that will last me for a good
long life to come."

And so we hurried forth and northward.

"Debby," said I, shortly, "Debby, upon my soul
you have fifty times the wit that I have."

"It does not need for you to tell me that, sir!" said
she. "Another instant and you would have said:
'Sir Officer, I am Merton Balfort, American, fighting
against his Majesty the King! Hang me if you like,
but remember that I am none of your British soldier,
nor yet a spy of that great monarch.'"

"Your pardon, mistress, 'his Majesty the King'?"

"Ah, dear sir," said she, bowing low in her saddle.

" 'T is my first lesson, eh? Pardon me. I should have said 'that dissolute monarch — er — man, George the Third.'"

"Debby," said I, "you are an angel! Will you draw your horse up and permit me to kiss your ladyship?"

"No, sir, I will not! I do not think I should allow it in any case just now, but certainly not upon the highway. And I wish you to understand, Merton Balfort, that I am not yet a rebel — er — that is, that George the Third is still the king."

"Yes, Mistress Balfort."

Up came her face towards me at the mention of her new name, and leaning over her horse she put her hand in mine, and said not a word as we rode along.

"I am too happy to stand it, Debby," said I, presently.

"Well, I should be happy too," said she, "if I knew how we were to live in the near future."

"If you think of that so seriously, why is it that all day you have been chuckling to yourself?"

"Oh, never mind! I have certain thoughts, and — and — certain knowledge of my own."

"Tell me."

"Not for the world."

"Tell me this instant! I am your husband."

"Sakes! You begin so soon, do you? Very well, then, listen to this: I will tell you not one single word! Now what doth thy noble husbandness say to that?"

"I say 't is outrageous and unwifely! But let it lie; for here are we come to the house where we may stay for the night, and that ends it."

It was the home of a man whom Atherton had
bidden us to by note, saying that we would get good
food and lodging, and no questions asked. And, indeed, we were in sore need of rest and comfort! I
had urged pushing on thus far that we might clear
the foul neutral country ahead of us the next day
while daylight held, and make the camp at Verplancks
by the next night. But, good horsewoman as Debby
was, she was nigh done for, and was more than willing to retire as soon as she had eaten.

Early in the morning we were again off, and, still
noting that my fair companion had something on her
mind, I was marvelling what it might be, when the
lay of the land along the road began to look familiar
and I recognised ahead of us the old tavern kept by
Gowan as it lay hiding itself under the hill. I turned
quickly to Debby and found her smiling mysteriously
at me.

" You know the spot? " I asked.

" Quite well," said she, " and I have a mind to stop,
and visit Master Gowan."

" Not by any means! " said I, decidedly. " The
place may be the house of our wedding, but just now
't is no place for you."

" And yet I would stop there a while, and — *will!* "
What a world of vigour was there in that last small
word!

I urged, commanded, — nay, tried force, — but to
no purpose. In we must go. So, dismounting, I
called for a hand to take our horses, and in we went
a second time to the dim old tavern.

20

Never shall I forget the little chuckle behind me as I stopped suddenly on the sill and saw — sitting as if in camp, perfectly at their ease — John Acton, with a huge pewter of ale before him, Robert Curtis — or Philipse, as he should be called — and, sitting at the same table between these two, that sombre old robber Marvin.

Up rose the three as I turned to Deborah and saw in an instant that she knew all — nay, that she had done the planning to bring it all about.

"Aha! Merton, my friend, here you be at last!" cried Acton, shaking us by the hand.

Curtis smiled quietly and gave me his friendly hand-clasp, and I had begun to express my surprise when Acton turned me about and cried:

"Here, man! Here is the Reverend James Marvin to welcome ye!"

"Marvin," said I, slowly, "you are a thieving scoundrel, and I have a mind to run this blade through your belly!"

"And yet," said the cool villain, "'t was I married ye to the girl ye would most have!"

"Married me, you scoundrel?" cried I. "Aye, at the point of a pistol!"

"And would ye have me undo it now?"

"That is none of your affair, man! Do you get out of here before I send you to the place where you belong!"

"Tut, tut! Merton," laughed Acton, "the Reverend Doctor is here by the special invitation of a lady."

I wheeled about and looked at Debby.

"You see, Merton, dear," — and for the first time since I had known her I believe she was a bit uneasy, — "you see I did not feel just sure I was really — you see — I did n't — "

"Feel quite sure whether she was Mistress Balfort, or Philipse, or king's subject, or rebel, or — "

"Merton," interrupted Curtis, "this was all arranged by Debby, and we are here to witness the wedding."

I looked again at her and found her brown eyes grown large with anxiety. And, for my sins, I caught the glint of a big tear ready to break loose at the first signal. What could a big fool like me do but take her hand and turn again to the scoundrel that, somehow, I could not feel much real anger against.

"Marvin, you thief," said I, "because of this fair lady you go free for this once. Do you marry me to her here and now! But if I ever run across you again, I'll slit you in two — I will, so help me — " But I could get no further, for even Curtis began to laugh at such a wedding.

And so there in that same grim room the old wretch did indeed marry us again, while Debby placed a hand that shook now a little in mine, and looked up at me as I had never known her to look at me before, with a faith and trust and gentleness that I swore to heaven should never go from her face and heart so long as I could give my poor life to keep them there. And beside us stood John Acton — serious, too, for the moment — and Robert Curtis Philipse, her brother, with a sadness upon him that nothing could ever lift, for that his life was seared by this war that had bereft him of all family ties. Deborah gave answer to the simple service in a low, gentle voice; and when we were done I kissed her for her brave heart and her dear self, and — be it confessed — in general thanks to God that she should come so freely to be with me for as long as He should give us life.

And so the little ceremony was done.

"Merton," said Curtis, as we sat down to some food, "I have a message for you that means much, I suspect," and he gave me a great official package that I knew came from headquarters as soon as my eye lit upon it. I was for letting it lie for the time, but Debby was for insisting on opening it to see what it might mean. And so I broke the seal, and found over our commander's great hand my appointment to be a major under dear old Putnam, and with this an order to join my regiment in Connecticut at once.

Acton slapped me on the back; Curtis gravely shook me by the hand; and Debby—aye, what would Debby do now?

"Will you go?" I asked.

"Why not, dear?" said she simply — as simply, as unhesitatingly as she has said the same thing every time from that day to this.

And so in the early afternoon I shook those two tried friends by the hand and bade them farewell, as we started riding eastward. Both were ordered South, to go they knew not where. Whether we three should ever meet again, no man could tell. But a higher authority decided that it should never be.

As I said when I began this egotistical scrawl, thirty years have gone since that day, and we have lived our life together till I have passed the half century. Our lot lay in camps for more than two years yet, and then peace and something that is even greater came to our devastated land; and peace and quiet came to Debby and to me. My lot has, after all, been a happy one, and I cannot complain.

Those two friends of mine went further and further southward, until at last they came with the great commander before the now historic village of Yorktown. There they saw and made part of the siege that gave us the right to say "American" before all the world. Acton returned in '83, and found us at home in Boston, where to this day he finds us still, — and where we sit together and smoke and talk of other days. But the other, Robert Curtis — as I always love to call him — stayed behind, lying for evermore in the trenches by that famous southern town.

THE END

CPSIA information can be obtained
at www.ICGtesting.com
Printed in the USA
LVHW081255240919
632112LV00014B/392/P